Making Assessment Matter

Also available from Continuum

Assessment, Lyn Overall and Margaret Sangster

Assessment: A Practical Guide for Secondary Teachers, Howard Turner and Sonia Jones

Making Assessment Matter

GRAHAM BUTT

continuum

Continuum International Publishing Group
The Tower Building, 11 York Road, London, SE1 7NX
80 Maiden Lane, Suite 704, New York, NY 10038

www.continuumbooks.com

© Graham Butt, 2010

British Library Cataloguing-in-Publication Data
A catalogue record for this book is available from the British Library.

ISBN: 978-1-84706-383-0 (paperback)

Library of Congress Cataloging-in-Publication Data
Butt, Graham.
 Making assessment matter / Graham Butt.
   p. cm.
 Includes bibliographical references.
 ISBN 978-1-84706-383-0
1. Educational tests and measurements. 2. Educational evaluation. I. Title.

 LB3051.B87 2009
 371.26--dc22

 2009034849

Typeset by Kenneth Burnley, Wirral, Cheshire
Printed and bound in Great Britain by . . .

Contents

Preface

Making Assessment Matter has been written to highlight the importance of the connections between teaching, learning and assessment. All of these activities should be interwoven and symbiotic, although in many classrooms and schools a curious dislocation occurs between them. The aim has been to clarify the reasons why assessment is central, perhaps even vital, to the act of learning, while also suggesting appropriate ways to improve the process of assessment. This book therefore explores the current place of assessment within our schools, with a particular focus on meeting the assessment needs of both the teacher and the student. The overall intention is to understand *why* assessment should matter.

Throughout this book the following themes are explored:

♦ The purposes of assessment.
♦ Using assessment to promote learning.
♦ The relationship between assessment and standards.
♦ 'High' and 'low' stakes assessment.
♦ Formative and summative assessment.
♦ Marking, feedback and self/peer assessment.
♦ Achieving assessment targets.
♦ Equality of opportunity and assessment.
♦ Making assessment easier (e-assessment).
♦ Wider assessment issues.

A number of associated concepts are covered, with the aim of bringing together considerations of 'high stakes' assessment at the national scale with day-to-day assessment practice in the classroom. *Making Assessment Matter* also poses four over-arching assessment questions which are addressed within and throughout the chapters:

◆ What is the nature of assessment in the context of state schooling and what directions should it now take?
◆ Does assessment, in whatever form, currently offer meaningful ways forward for the educational development of the learner?
◆ What is the role of the state with respect to educational assessment?
◆ How can best assessment practice be supported and promoted in schools?

Because assessment is very much part of the whole routine of education, many teachers realize that it is inextricably linked to their professional practice – it is not an 'add-on', it is not optional, it is not insignificant. Nonetheless, formal assessment has traditionally been treated as a somewhat 'separate' activity, sitting outside the normal realms of daily teaching and learning (Butt 2005a). This separateness has been exacerbated by the very nature of 'high stakes' assessment practice, primarily conducted through public examinations away from the direct control of the teacher and the school. In such assessment, candidates' scripts are sent from the school to an external body which then marks them, grades them (in some way) and reports back the results to the candidates – usually at the end of a course or unit of study. This has reinforced the importance of summative assessment processes, which are largely out of the control of the classroom teacher.

The current re-focusing of assessment practice in the National Curriculum towards the day-to-day formative assessment of students, primarily for educational rather than bureaucratic purposes, has already had a significant impact on much classroom-based assessment. If assessment is integral to all teaching and learning, it is therefore also central to planning, preparation and target setting. Formative assessment methods strive to achieve such centrality within the education process. Unfortunately, as Carr (2008) reminds us, 'learning outcomes are fuzzy and learning settings are messy' (p. 36) – our assessment practices have to be sophisticated if we are to accurately measure what we hope to measure.

The title of this book, which is intentionally somewhat ambiguous, might imply that assessment has *not* mattered in the past – that it is something that only now requires our attention to give it greater significance: literally, to make it 'matter'. Many would argue that this is simply not the case, for 'high stakes' summative assessment has surely always mattered. Indeed, it seems to have exerted a disproportionate influence on national educational policy and practice for many years. Assessment is currently the cornerstone on which state education in most developed countries is built. While the importance of 'high stakes' assessment is not disputed – we could not run our national education systems without its awarding, certification and selection functions, and we currently rely hugely on its provision of data – the significance of day-to-day formative assessment in developing the learner is less well appreciated. Here is arguably where we should strive to make assessment matter, for educational rather than bureaucratic reasons. Despite recent government interest in the role of Assessment for Learning (AfL), the inspection reports of the Office for Standards in Education (OfSTED) still regularly comment that teachers have significant improvements to make in their assessment practices. *Making Assessment Matter* has a further, connected meaning, in that the title also refers to the act of creating something (or 'making matter') – that is, constructing materials, approaches and strategies to assist in our educational assessment.

Each of the chapters in *Making Assessment Matter* introduces the reader to a range of ideas, some of which I have already discussed within various professional and academic publications. In this respect I am particularly indebted to Chris Kington, of Chris Kington Publications, for allowing me to draw substantially upon assessment articles I have previously published in the journals *Into Teaching* and *Into Teaching – the induction year* (Optimus Publishing), as the basis for sections of many of the chapters. Chapter 8 is similarly structured around an article previously published by myself, Phil Wood and Paul Weeden on boys' underachievement published in the journal *International Research in Geographical and Environmental Education* in 2004 (Butt *et al.* 2004). Figure 2.1 originally appeared in Weeden et al. (2002, p. 23) and is reproduced here by kind permission of RoutledgeFalmer. As a geography educator, much of my work on assessment has been undertaken within this community which is reflected in the nature of the references for this book.

I am indebted to the school students, trainee teachers, early career teachers and academic colleagues who have influenced my thinking and supported me over the years with respect to a variety of assessment matters. The Geographical Association's Assessment and Examinations Working Group, of which I have been a member for over 25 years, has been particularly influential. Also my colleague Paul Weeden, who kindly agreed to comment on a draft of this book, has remained a constant source of ideas and information on all matters related to assessment.

I remain convinced that assessment is essentially an art, not a science. The potential of formative assessment to shape, direct and stimulate the educational progress of young people is fundamental to my beliefs about assessment. Much of my professional life has been dedicated to working with new teachers – this has almost certainly influenced the style in which this book is written, as well as the nature of some of its content. However, I believe that there is much here that will be of interest to the experienced teacher, the policy-maker and other academics who will hopefully find the blend of theory and practice suitable to their needs.

1 | Introducing assessment

Assessment is, and always has been, fundamentally important to the whole process of education. Indeed, it is increasingly being called upon to deliver a widening variety of educational and bureaucratic functions, some of which sit uneasily with the accepted principles of assessment practice.

Assessment should be integral to the acts of teaching and learning. It can be used to support student progression, and its findings can be applied to establish educational goals and targets. The impacts of different assessment practices on learning can be positive, negative or benign – serving either to encourage or demotivate the learner. National assessment data is collected annually, in the form of 'high stakes' external examination results, to construct measurements of how well students, teachers and schools are performing. Over the past two decades in the United Kingdom the use of such data has achieved a certain elevation and prominence, although arguably it commands a much greater importance than it truly warrants. Assessment is both a day-to-day activity for teachers and a large-scale, profitable industry for the examination awarding bodies – providing a focus for the educational concerns of parents, politicians and the media (Swaffield 2008). The significance given to the processes and outcomes of assessment, particularly with respect to the standards that exist in our schools, is greater now than at any time in the past.

All teachers spend a considerable proportion of their working lives assessing students' work. In a national survey of teacher workload, secondary school teachers in England reported spending up to 22 per cent of their week engaged in aspects of monitoring, assessing, recording and reporting – commenting that the assessment activities they undertook were often overly bureaucratic and served to lower their morale (see Butt and Lance 2005). If assessment is so beneficial to our students' education, why are teachers seemingly so negative towards it, and many students so dismissive of the educational feedback it can provide? Arguably, both teachers and students need to be clearer about the purposes of assessing, the best assessment procedures to adopt, and the ways to maximize the positive impacts of assessment.

But what do we mean by 'assessment'? The term has very wide usage within education, but it is regularly applied without clear definition. Assessment can refer to something as seemingly mundane as the teacher's daily use of oral 'question and answer' within the classroom – where each student's response provides the teacher with a little more information about their abilities and attainment – to the grander scale, final, external examinations which candidates sit for their Standard Assessment Tasks (SATs), General Certificates of Secondary Education (GCSEs), Advanced Subsidiary (AS) or Advanced level (A level) examinations. These are the two ends of a continuum across which lies a huge range of both formal and informal assessment activity, the bulk of which often involves teachers marking written work produced by their students in response to classroom- or home-work-based tasks. Stobart (2008) recognizes that the terms 'assessment', 'examinations' and 'tests' are often used interchangeably – although he acknowledges that 'assessment' usually encompasses a range of approaches to evidence gathering; 'examinations' refers to open-ended (written) responses under standardized conditions; and 'tests' can include the use of multiple-choice instruments. What we do with the outcomes of assessment is a key consideration – not least whether assessment evidence, gathered by whatever means, always has to be formally recorded. Does each piece of assessed work warrant entering a mark or comment in a mark book (or in an electronic file) as a score or grade, or can some assessment information be left as ephemeral evidence which the teacher mentally stores away? Is assessment only valid, reliable and useful if it is formally recorded? Or does the very act of constantly recording student performance change the ways in which students and teachers respond to the act of assessment?

This leads us to a big question: What is assessment *for*? Is it simply to gain a set of grades (or scores, or percentages, or comments) to sum up what each student has achieved, or is it a means of enabling students to take their next educational steps with confidence – or both? With this question in mind Dylan Wiliam (2008) reminds us of the many purposes to which assessment is put:

It is through assessment that we can find out whether students have learned what they have been taught, so that we can make appropriate adjustments to our teaching. Assessments are used to describe the achievements of students, so that decisions can be made about their suitability for particular jobs, or the kinds of educational experiences that should follow. Parents use the results of assessments to learn about the progress their children are making at school, and to make decisions about the quality of education offered in different schools. And, of course, policy-makers use assessments to provide information about the quality of schools and curricula. (p. 123)

Furthermore, Stobart (2008) indicates a number of key historical roles for assessment, in addition to its use in identifying ability and merit, when he describes its functions as follows:

> . . . establishing authenticity in pre-scientific times; certificating occupational competence through the guilds and professions; identifying learners in need of special schooling or provision; and as an accountability tool to judge the effectiveness of institutions. (p. 13)

Assessment has previously been succinctly defined as 'the process of gathering, interpreting, recording and using information about students' responses to educational tasks' (Lambert and Lines 2000). As such, assessment has several goals – first, to provide feedback to teachers and students about each child's progress in order to support their future learning (a formative role); second, to produce information about the level of student achievement (a summative role); third, to offer a means of selecting students for further courses and/or employment (a certification role); and fourth, to help judge the effectiveness of the education system (an evaluative role). Achieving a clear understanding of these different purposes, and about whether they can be combined successfully, is enormously important for practising teachers (Butt 2005a).

Assessment as measurement

Essentially assessment is about measurement: primarily the measurement of student performance against a particular task, or tasks. Once some form of measurement has taken place we need to do something meaningful with the information that has been gained. This can involve target setting and supporting the student, or simply (for now) recording and reporting assessment data for future reference. What frustrates many teachers is the fact that although they generate considerable amounts of assessment data, much of this is not used to gain any significant advance in student learning, or in their own teaching. Unfortunately the target setting that is associated with test results often has a distorting effect on teaching and learning – targets may yield short-term benefits, but ultimately undermine effective education as teachers and students simply learn how to 'play the system' (Stobart 2008). This reinforces the fundamental importance of the question 'What are we assessing *for*?' and whether assessment practices can be changed to make them more useful to both teachers and learners. The issue of who the prime audience is – students, teachers, parents, bureaucrats, or other stakeholders – and whether the ways in which assessment data are used for managerial and accountability purposes are valid, reliable and fit for purpose, also need to be considered.

Assessment practice in schools

The recent history of assessment practice in schools is revealing. If we consider what has happened in schools in England and Wales over the past twenty years (which largely parallels the shifts in assessment practices in many other developed countries), these trends highlight changes in the purposes to which we put assessment.

The National Curriculum, which was introduced into English and Welsh state schools following the passing of the 1988 Education Reform Act, has had a profound effect on assessment practice in schools. It heralded the increased centralization of control of assessment, not least as before the National Curriculum was launched, 'high stakes' public assessment had only occurred at the ages of 16, 17 and 18 for most students (at GSCE, Advanced Subsidiary and Advanced level) – although in those Local Authorities (LAs) that retained grammar schools, external assessment also occurred at age 11 (the 11+ examination) as a means of selection. In tandem with the introduction of the National Curriculum subjects came new, externally assessed tests called the Standard Assessment Tasks (SATs) – initially at the ages of 7, 11 and 14, but now almost entirely abandoned – for the core subjects of Mathematics, Science and English. Teacher assessments were to be carried out in all the other subjects. Each of these assessments took place at the end of the first three Key Stages of the National Curriculum, with GCSEs fulfilling the assessment role at the end of Key Stage 4. The amount of formal assessment of students was therefore radically increased with the introduction of the National Curriculum, making children in England and Wales the focus of considerable over-assessment.

The centralization of assessment was undertaken for a number of reasons. First, it meant that the National Curriculum could provide national assessment information annually for the government on the performance of students, teachers and schools. Second, it created a baseline of assessment data from which national standards and targets for performance could be set. Third, it enabled more fine-grained measurement of educational performance which, when combined with inspection evidence, offered a fuller picture of those schools and LAs in which student achievement was highest and lowest, improving or levelling off. This data highlighted where action would be needed to raise performance. At face value, centralizing assessment sounds very sensible, positive and even laudable – who would not want to have such data to help improve performance? However, the difficulties of trying to match assessment information to real improvements in student performance are legend. Add to this the arguments surrounding the creation of league tables of school performance, the veracity or otherwise of 'adding value' to the achievement levels of children, the questionable effects on teaching and learning in schools, and the debate about what 'standards' actually are (or should be), and the picture becomes much less clear.

It was apparent by the early 1990s that the National Curriculum – and the teaching and learning that was associated with it – had become dangerously 'assessment driven'. The introduction of high stakes assessments at the end of each Key Stage skewed the work of teachers and students towards preparation for the next set of tests or teacher assessments, while also incurring massive costs to the state for the production, administration and marking of the

SATs. The first major reform of the National Curriculum and its assessment came in 1995, led by Sir Ron Dearing, with the aim of reducing the content-driven nature of many of the subjects. Even so, in assessment terms, these initial reforms were modest, for the principle of using assessment evidence to lever up standards nationally was still attractive to the government of the day. The annual comparison of schools and teachers on the basis of national assessment evidence continues, despite the subsequent removal of SATs testing entirely from Wales and at the culmination of Key Stage 3 in England. Towards the end of the first decade of the twenty-first century, SATs testing has essentially been abandoned in English schools, with only Mathematics and English tests remaining for 10- and 11-year-olds. Teacher assessment was mooted as a suitable replacement for such tests.

One positive result of Dearing's reforms of the National Curriculum was the early realization that the use of expensive 'pencil and paper' tests across the whole curriculum was not feasible. This meant that teachers had to become more adept at teacher assessment – specifically, the assessment of their students' performance against set criteria known as level descriptions. By introducing a national system of criterion-referenced assessment, a radical change in assessment practice was initiated. This was positive in that students who traditionally performed poorly in test situations no longer had to cross as many of these particular hurdles. However, attempting to standardize teacher assessments nationally was something new and untried. For many teachers, particularly those in primary schools, providing a level for each of their student's attainment at the end of each of the Key Stages proved challenging. The levels were chosen from eight levels of attainment (the level descriptions) for each foundation subject, essentially a process of criterion-referenced assessment, with the level descriptions being the criteria which established the national standards of performance. The obvious issue was, and still is, the consistency with which teachers make their judgements – for example, is teacher A's assessment of a particular child's attainment the same as teacher B's? Would the same work, performance and evidence of attainment be assessed similarly by these two teachers, or indeed any other teacher? Lip service is paid to the equivalence of teacher assessment and national testing, but are these equally valid, reliable and fit for purpose?

What has become evident is that the use of assessment information is central to the effective planning, organization and evaluation of lessons. There are convincing arguments that can be advanced about the importance of placing assessment at the centre of the process of teaching and learning – not least that it is only by the teacher measuring (assessing) the learning that children have attained during a lesson that he or she will know what the next learning step should be. Therefore, the day-to-day process of lesson planning must inevitably be tied to the ongoing assessment of student performance – without this, how does one know what should be taught next? Without accurate information on what students have attained, what they have struggled with, what they need more time to learn, and where they should go next – all gathered as assessment evidence – their learning cannot advance. There must be a close correlation between what we, as teachers, teach and what children, as learners, learn.

Unfortunately, as the Qualifications and Curriculum Authority (QCA)-funded LEARN project identified at the end of the last century, many students remain unclear about what they are learning, why they are learning it and how this learning will be assessed. They are uncertain about their own strengths and weaknesses as learners and do not have clear ideas about how to improve – relying heavily on their teachers to guide their learning (Weeden *et al.* 2002). Little appears to have changed since the late 1990s. Students may perform better year on year in formal assessments, but essentially they appear to be no more empowered as independent learners than in previous generations.

In a landmark paper which reviewed published research on teacher assessment, Black and Wiliam (1998a) concluded that student learning responded most positively to frequent formative assessment. Equally important, they believed, was the ability of students to reflect honestly on their own academic performance and picture their learning in terms of what is needed for them to perform better. Unfortunately, day-to-day assessment practices in classrooms often reveal the following shortcomings:

◆ Superficial rote learning often takes place, with classroom assessment based on the recall of details of knowledge which students soon forget.
◆ Teachers fail to review the forms of assessment used, do not discuss assessment practices with other teachers and rarely reflect on what is being assessed.

◆ There is an over-emphasis on grading and an under-emphasis on learning.
◆ There is a tendency to use normative rather than criterion referenced assessment systems.
◆ Teachers emphasize competition through their assessment methods, rather than personal achievement and performance.
◆ Assessment methods tend to reinforce perceptions of failure among the less able, leading to de-motivation and a loss of confidence in their ability to learn.
◆ Dominance of external, summative testing is still the norm. (After Black and Wiliam 1998b)

Black *et al.* (2003) have also found that the general problems related to assessment can be broadly divided into three categories – those concerned with effective learning; those concerned with negative impact; and those which focused on the managerial role of assessment. In essence, effective learning is diminished because testing encourages rote and superficial learning; assessment methods are not discussed or critically reviewed among teachers in schools; and quantity and presentation of work are emphasized to the neglect of its quality. The negative impact of assessment, exacerbated by the over-emphasis on awarding grades and the under-provision of useful advice, reinforces a lack of emphasis on the role of learning. In addition, students are regularly compared with each other in terms of assessed performance rather than focusing on personal improvement, leading to the demotivation of low-attaining students. Finally, the managerial role of assessment tends to dominate, rather than that related to learning. Often teachers can predict their students' likely performance on external tests, usually because their own assessment regimes closely imitate these, but they are less aware of their students' learning needs. Superficial learning, as opposed to deep learning, abounds.

The influence of public examinations

Some form of externally validated, 'public' or 'high stakes' examination has been part of the organized systems of education in most economically developed countries from their very origins. In the United Kingdom the provision of state education has been paralleled by the creation of systems of assessing, certificating, awarding and accred iting young people who have completed their courses of study. The historical and cultural legacy of assessment is important: written examinations originated in élite universities and spread to the professions and secondary schools, influencing examination systems to the present day (Stobart 2008). English examination boards were originally created by universities from the mid-nineteenth century onwards, to establish standards in schools and to measure the achievement of middle-class boys. Remnants of these systems are enduring; for example, at the time of writing, Advanced level (A level) qualifications have existed within the British education system for almost 60 years and still represent the 'gold standard' qualification for assessing student attainment at age 18. In various forms these qualifications also serve many Commonwealth countries, where young people still sit 'overseas' versions of the A level which have been tailored (some more successfully than others) to their national context.

In recent years, the external examination system has changed significantly. Back in 1986 the two-tier system of examinations at 16 was ended by the introduction of the General Certificate of Secondary Education (GCSE), which effectively combined the previous Certificate of Secondary Education (CSE) and the Ordinary level (O level) examination. This examination purported to serve up to 80 per cent of the ability range of the 16+ cohort, often through the use of 'tiered' papers geared to 'high' or 'low' ability candidates, rather than having two examinations for the purpose.

The question of an appropriate examination, or other means of assessment for those young people who do not wish to follow an academic route in the latter years of their education has always been a thorny one for the British education system. The main stumbling block has been the comparability of academic and vocational courses and their assessment. Here we confront major issues of esteem and status, often bordering on the verge of prejudice. With the dominance of academic routes through education, linked to pervasive philosophies of education which elevated the liberal humanist traditions of schooling, the introduction of vocational courses and qualifications has always proved problematic. For the British, the academic route has always represented the most highly valued, prestigious and cultured pathway for young people, while routes associated with vocationalism and 'knowing how to' have been seen as the lot of those less fortunate individuals who were not quite bright, or able enough to carry away the glittering prizes. This is not the case throughout many European nations, nor in many other economically developed countries, where the abilities and talents of gifted young people find more equal recognition, status and parity of esteem in vocational arenas.

Conclusions

We have seen that assessment is now a cornerstone of our educational practice. In England and Wales the National Curriculum was designed with assessment in mind, alongside an established and respected system of 'high stakes' public examinations. Subsequently the government, partly through its National Strategies, has placed an increasing emphasis on Assessment for Learning (AfL). However, 'high stakes' public examinations have generally dominated and distorted assessment practices in schools: 'There is more to learning than examination grades, yet, for policy-makers, "raising standards" is often simply about better grades' (Stobart 2008, p. 16).

For each teacher, assessment must be a major consideration in his or her daily regime of planning, teaching and evaluation. If the act of assessment is applied as an afterthought to lesson or curriculum planning, children will not progress appropriately. Experienced teachers understand the central role that assessment plays in effective education, skilfully using different forms of assessment (formative, summative, diagnostic and evaluative) to support the whole process of teaching and learning. They use their professional judgement to apply different assessment methods and techniques that are appropriate to their task – to do so with confidence and competence takes time and experience. It is dangerous to make the mistake of assuming that objective assessment systems exist which one simply has to apply to produce infallible, accurate measurements of students' abilities and attainment. To try to do so places an unrealistic expectation on any assessment system. Not only are many forms of assessment wrongly applied, resulting in 'user error' affecting the validity of the results, but they are often used with unrealistic expectations of what they can achieve. Fine-tuning assessment methods to our needs is a skill. No assessment methods are infallible.

Ultimately, our view of the value of assessment – what it is capable of doing, what it can offer the teacher and the learner, and how central it is to the process of education – is heavily influenced by our view of intelligence. Some teachers believe that intelligence is largely fixed and pre-determined genetically; their view is that education can do little to change this situation. For these teachers, assessment simply provides a means of (re)measuring the extent of their students' abilities year on year. However, other teachers believe that intelligence is not fixed and immutable, but capable of further development and growth. As such, assessment can help to map an educational pathway which incrementally helps the child to develop, pushing his or her abilities, attainment and understanding further and further. Here, the results of student assessment are not pre-determined, but open to teachers making a difference (Butt 2005a). Our educational values and beliefs are therefore important. We (should) choose to assess what we value most in our children's education – a process which is necessarily determined by our views of what is important in teaching and learning and about children's abilities to learn and their potential to achieve. Assessment should be an expression of what we value, underpinned by what we believe about the educability of children. Here educators such as Hart *et al.* (2004), Drummond (2008) and Chitty (2001) question the assumptions that children are born with a fixed quota of 'intelligence', which remains fixed through childhood and into adult life. They reject rigid notions of 'ability' and 'predictability' which are currently integral to formal assessment frameworks – along with 'the apparatus of levels, targets and standards' (Drummond 2008, p. 17) – replacing them with the concept of learning *capacity*. What is important here is that we can only have confidence in the assessment methods we apply if they achieve validity within our framework of understanding learning. There is a danger that if the methods of assessment lose contact with the underpinning theories of learning they will lose their validity. When assessment methods and techniques lose sight of what learning is, and what type of learning we believe our students should engage with, they become useless.

2 | Using assessment to promote learning

Stobart (2008) asserts that:

> Being clear about the purpose of an assessment is an essential, although often neglected, first step. Is it about establishing what needs to be learned; about what has been learned; about classroom control . . . ; or about managerial control, for example, the half-termly test required by the school? A good follow-up question may be: *How necessary is this assessment*? (p. 102)

As we have seen in Chapter 1, assessment should be placed at the very centre of the act of teaching and learning – our ideas about how students learn, how we plan lessons, how we choose our assessment methods and our concepts of intelligence should all connect. Currently the assumed good practice when using assessment to promote learning is tied to methods of formative assessment, or 'Assessment for Learning' (AfL).

Formative assessment promises a lot. It claims to be able to improve the quality of what students learn and challenges many previously accepted assessment practices. Our adoption of the theories and principles of formative assessment is therefore an act of embracing change and questioning assumptions about 'what works' in assessment terms. However, we must be convinced that research evidence can back up the beliefs that formative assessment promotes learning and raises achievement. In this chapter, I want to start to explore how formative assessment connects to current learning theory, student motivation and to the planning of classroom-based assessment. In Chapters 4 and 5, the similarities and differences between formative/'low stakes' and summative/'high stakes' assessment methods are considered in more depth, widening the focus beyond the classroom.

Gathering evidence

Reference has already been made to the work of Paul Black and Dylan Wiliam who published a major review of research into formative assessment at the end of the 1990s (Black and Wiliam 1998a). On the basis of their review of 250 pieces of research literature, they concluded that frequent feedback from the teacher to the learner, using assessment evidence, can 'yield substantial learning gains' (p. 7). That is, by using formative assessment methods teachers can bring about measurable improvements in student performance. They estimated that during the two years normally spent studying for a GCSE, students should be capable of improving their performance by one or two grades if formative assessment methods are used in the classroom on a regular basis. These are very significant expectations – particularly when one considers the prospect of 'less able' students achieving 'good' GCSE grades, rather than leaving school stigmatized as academic failures. Their research also suggests that low-attaining students have the most to gain from the application of formative assessment methods, highlighting the possibilities of real academic achievement for these learners.

Successfully gathering research evidence about the benefits of using particular forms of assessment to promote learning is never easy (Butt 2006a). By its very nature successful formative assessment, in the words of both Sadler (1989) and Lambert (1996), relies on teachers 'getting to know' their students better. Researching this is problematic – much assessment information held by teachers is highly personal, based on their unique knowledge of each student's particular strengths and weaknesses: what the child seems to find 'easy', what motivates or frustrates them, which tasks excite them, what they will 'struggle on with' and when they will give up. Much of this information teachers carry around in their heads. It is therefore information which researchers find very difficult to extract and analyse in an objective way. An additional problem is that we do not all use the same terminology to describe ostensibly similar phenomena. For example, 'formative assessment' can be referred to by teachers as 'Assessment for Learning', 'classroom assessment', 'teacher assessment', 'feedback', 'feedforward', 'student-centred assessment' and 'formative evaluation'. It can be argued that each of these terms has a very specific meaning within the broad umbrella of formative assessment and therefore should not be used interchangeably. This is not merely a moot point for the researcher – if we wish to understand something we need to define our terms, or else we run the risk of wrongly interpreting information (Butt 2006a).

To start from an 'even base' let us accept the definition of formative assessment proposed by the Assessment Reform Group (ARG):

> . . . the process of seeking and interpreting evidence for use by learners and their teachers to decide where the learners are in their learning, where they need to go and how best to get there. (ARG 1999)

The connection between theories of learning and assessment

Arguably, the learning theory within which formative assessment sits most comfortably is social constructivist theory. Drawing on aspects of the work of Dewey (1916), Vygotsky (1962), Bruner (1961) and Piaget (1954), the constructivist model assumes that learning does not occur as a simple linear act – that is, the learner does not move steadily and inexorably forward in the acquisition of knowledge, understanding and skills. Rather, learning is sporadic: some things are learnt quickly and easily, others take more time and effort. Learning is both a social and a cultural activity, where the learner actively constructs his or her own meanings as a result of exposure to a variety of educational experiences. Much of our learning is short term, or surface, in nature; some is more long term, or deep. Social constructivist theory assumes that we place our new understandings into the context of what we knew before – changing some of the foundations of what we previously knew, to make way for fresh concepts and ideas. The term 'scaffolding' – used to express the ways in which the teacher can skilfully support the learning that students achieve as they 'construct' new knowledge and understanding – is relevant here.

If we believe that at the heart of formative assessment is a need to 'get to know' our students better, it seems logical that assessment evidence should help us to do so and construct better learning activities. We can only appreciate what such activities might be with the aid of assessment information, which will inform us about the next educational steps students should take. This raises another, fundamentally important, aspect of constructivist thinking – that most learning in schools is essentially an *interactive* process, where both teacher and learner bring something to the educational table. Each agent has their own conceptions, ideas, beliefs, information and understandings which need to be communicated to the other if learning is to occur. This is certainly not a simple transmission–reception model of teaching and learning. Here learning is advanced by using assessment information, supported by the teacher setting targets and establishing educational 'next steps' with the students. Achieving real learning is therefore not seen simply as a function of memorization and testing.

Traditional views of assessment, which are often based on the belief that students are 'empty vessels' to be filled with knowledge, usually assume the following:

◆ Learning should be individually assessed, and any influence by others in the assessment process is 'cheating'.
◆ Assessment is focused on performance under test conditions.
◆ Assessment relies on the student demonstrating an ability to recall facts and/or demonstrate skills.
◆ Tests are used at the end of a course or sequence of learning, and are separate from the learning episodes.
◆ Preparation for tests involves practice (such as using past papers).
◆ Tests are time limited; the speed of completion indicates how well learning is established.
◆ No access to materials is allowed as knowledge or skill is expected to be memorized or established.
◆ Questions are organized in a hierarchy of difficulty, starting with the least difficult (often as short answer or multiple-choice questions).
◆ Assessed responses provide a score enabling comparisons with other learners (norm-referenced), or against a standard (criterion-referenced), or both.
◆ It may be possible to infer areas for improvement from returned marked scripts. (Adapted from James 2008a, p. 24)

James (2008a) refers to these as 'first generation' assessment practices, which characterize the assessment of learning within a transmission–reception model of education.

'Second generation' assessment practice, or assessing learning as individual 'sense making', is somewhat different. Here the focus is still on the individual acquiring knowledge and skills, but the conception of the learning process has shifted. Active learning is seen as an important facet of students making their own meaning, where the students mediate what is learnt from what is taught (they do not learn *everything* they are taught in the way the teacher might expect). Here assessment is not merely about testing factual recall. The assessment principles that link these constructivist views of learning have similarities to, but also some key differences from, the traditional 'first generation' assessment practices:

◆ Importance of problem-solving and understanding stressed.
◆ Assessment is focused on student performance when finding solutions to problems and demonstrating cognitive skills.
◆ Tasks/tests may be extended to allow those being assessed to show the breadth and depth of their understanding, or to solve complex problems (concept maps, open-ended assessments, projects, coursework, etc. may be preferred forms of assessment).
◆ Limited access given to materials, as assessment is less a test of memory than one of understanding.
◆ Responses to tasks/problems according to specified criteria requiring the assessor to make a judgement, as more than one acceptable answer may be possible. This requires moderation procedures to develop a conception of appropriate standards.
◆ Assumption of progression against levels, grades or a 'ladder' of scores, assuming a trajectory of progress can be described.
◆ Improvement assumed from 'novice' to 'expert' performance.
◆ Areas for improvement implied from failures/misunderstandings in solving problems. Certain ideas may need to be unlearned, or new cognitive skills developed. (Adapted from James 2008a, p. 27)

The constructivist model of learning, and its associated assessment processes, implies that teachers assist individual students in constructing new meanings by positioning what is taught within a framework of what they already know. Unlike first generation (learning and) assessment practices, students are not seen as receivers of discrete bundles of knowledge transmitted by the teacher, but as actively developing their knowledge and understanding from what is taught. This implies assessment and feedback is a two way process – with teachers needing to know, understand and build on what students have already attained.

Third generation assessment practice, according to James (2008a), adopts a socio-cultural approach to learning which stresses the importance of knowledge being built among other learners (sometimes referred to as 'situated' learning). This steps beyond the behaviourist assumptions of first generation assessment, and the cognitive, individualist approach of second generation practices, to focus on the importance of interaction with others when learning. Here, learning within social groups who share a common language of knowledge and understanding is important. Theoretical foundations are rooted in the work of educational psychologists such as Vygotsky, Piaget, Bruner and Engeström.

In assessment terms, the implications of James' work must be somewhat tentative, mainly because many of the socio-cultural theories are relatively new and focus on learning rather than assessment. However, he attempts to provide some pointers:

◆ Assessment should be 'situated'. If learning cannot be separated from the actions that generate it, then assessment should also be embedded in the learning process – not carried out as a 'bolt on' after the learning event.

◆ Assessment needs to be done by the learning community, not external assessors. This implies a key role for self, peer and teacher assessment. Group learning as well as individual learning should be assessed.

◆ Most appropriate forms of assessment involve problem-solving, addressing 'real world' problems (which are encountered in the learning process).

◆ Use of resources is important, for this shows agency in the ways in which individuals and groups use what is available to them (materials, human resources, intellectual capital, etc.). Assessment of how people approach problem-solving, work together and evaluate their actions is key, suggesting a concentration on collaborative and project work, or coursework-type assessments.

◆ Judgements should be qualitative, rather than quantitative, to fit the socio-cultural approach. (Adapted from James 2008a, p. 31)

There are obviously complexities, particularly as third generation assessment practice implies greater assessment of groups of learners, rather than individuals, where the tracking of 'who has done what' is much more complicated. The fact that learning is co-constructed with others, with students learning from each other as well as the teacher, implies that assessment and feedback should be a genuinely open and flexible process – where students may initiate and shape the assessment dialogue as much as the teacher.

In essence, the *process* of formative assessment is seen by many teachers as being as important as the *product* (the marks or grades that result). The location of assessment in the act of learning is therefore seen as central, rather than peripheral, to each student's education. Assessment information is used to help students understand what they currently do well and what they do badly, how to address any problems they have, and what realistic targets might be set for both teacher and learner to make the process of learning more successful in future.

Assessment as intelligence testing

Claims that assessment can be used to measure ability with any degree of accuracy are doubtful – we may be able to assess achievement and attainment, but find the assessment of ability far more problematic. Previous use of IQ testing claimed that such tests were socially and culturally neutral, enabling the tester to gain an objective measurement of each child's ability. These tests were applied to predict future performance and therefore to make decisions about who should be granted the opportunity to access particular types of education – the use of 11+ examinations in the UK as a means of selecting those who should progress to grammar schools on the basis of their verbal reasoning and arithmetical competence, is an example of this. Selection served to strengthen divisions and created self-fulfilling prophecies – tests were used to identify differences in ability, students were accordingly sent to different types of schools (academic, technical), and the education that they subsequently received served to cement these original differences. The implication that education can have little effect in shifting ability, particularly when this is perceived as 'given', 'innate' and 'immutable', is obviously damaging. Intelligence testing as the basis for selection of this sort is therefore neither objective nor fair.

Motivational aspects

Educational psychologists have highlighted the importance of motivation to learning. Assessment can have a huge motivational (or demotivational) impact on students: after all, learning is not just an intellectual process, it is also an emotional and personal one. We have all felt the elation of receiving positive assessment feedback – and the sense of dejection, humiliation and defeat that is a consequence of the opposite! Such feedback may seem like a judgement not only on the work we have produced, but also on ourselves as individuals. Depending on our resilience, this may have a significant impact on our continued effort and application – students who constantly experience feelings of rejection, alienation and dissatisfaction as a result of assessment feedback often simply give up. Good assessment practice is clearly connected to principles of good teaching. It should be motivational, empowering, encouraging and confidence-building. The act of assessment is also an act of labelling. Whether overt or implicit, there is a danger that we may fall into a trap of simplistically labelling learners as being of either 'high' or 'low' ability; usually in relation to their assessed performance. This can be pejorative, narrowly ascribing qualities (or a *lack* of qualities) to the learner which may be inappropriate, inaccurate or unfair. If we only measure student performance against assessment criteria, we may not achieve a full appreciation of the range of each child's abilities. This can be exacerbated in assessment systems that value the written word, for we all know of students who only perform well orally, revealing an ability level they can not reproduce on paper.

Schools have a duty to maximize the potential of all their children. Unfortunately the lowest attaining students often respond less successfully to initiatives designed to improve their learning. This can link directly to low levels of student motivation which remain hard to shift. Students quickly realize the significance of having been divided from their peers into different teaching groups, or of having different work set on the evidence of their assessed performances. When students are streamed or banded the highest achievers generally have their positive motivation towards school and learning reinforced, while the lowest attainers see little return for their efforts and lose motivation. It is easy to classify students into those who are 'well motivated' on the basis of their success in assessments – gaining the confidence to try new challenges, take risks and be reasonably assured of success. Those who lose motivation because they always seem to fail, or think they are not clever enough, find few ways forward and therefore tend to give up (Tunstall and Gipps 1996). There are, of course, strong links to whether one sees intelligence levels as largely fixed and persistent, or flexible and capable of improvement.

Weeden *et al.* (2002), with reference to the work of Shirley Clarke (2001), note that some students' poor motivation presents itself as 'learned helplessness', where a history of educational failure means that these students refuse to engage with academic work. Such students often integrate poorly with their peers and may present social and behavioural issues. Solutions may involve making learning more relevant to their needs, appealing to more utilitarian aspects of education by changing the curriculum, and assessing more positively through formative assessment to avoid labelling these students as failures. Importantly, achievement, and therefore motivation, is context-specific – there are plenty of situations in which we may feel uncertain and where we fear that we might perform badly. For those children for whom academic work is difficult – where their performance usually reinforces a sense of their own failure – motivation will always be poor. Hence the careless labelling of children as being of 'low ability' (or 'high ability') should be avoided, as ability levels can vary according to task and motivation.

All teachers have a duty to assess their students. However, the extent to which teachers use assessment to support the *learning* of their students, or merely to record their progress, varies from teacher to teacher. We must acknowledge the importance of adopting formative assessment strategies and of helping students develop a better understanding of self-assessment, as a means of extending their appreciation of how they learn. Teachers play a central role in assessment, with students usually relying very heavily on their teachers' feedback – which is often informal, sometimes unintentional – to determine how they are doing. Assessment practices therefore have clear connections to aspects of students' motivation and self-esteem. The process of assessment obviously has consequences for future learning. When teachers adapt their pedagogy in an attempt to improve the learning experiences of their students using assessment evidence as a foundation for change, this is 'assessment for learning' (AfL).

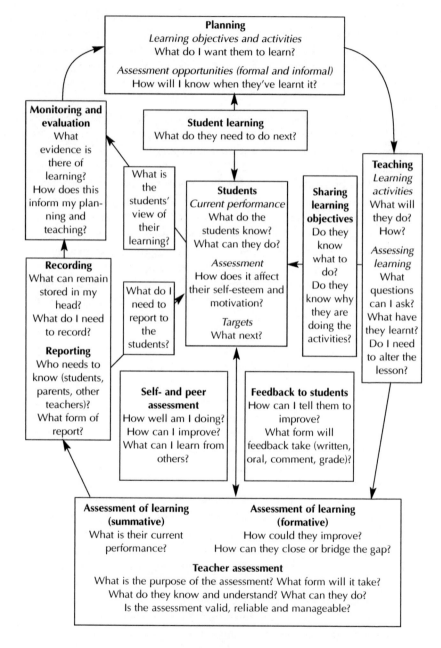

Planning
Learning objectives and activities
What do I want them to learn?

Assessment opportunities (formal and informal)
How will I know when they've learnt it?

Monitoring and evaluation
What evidence is there of learning?
How does this inform my planning and teaching?

Student learning
What do they need to do next?

What is the students' view of their learning?

Teaching
Learning activities
What will they do?
How?

Assessing learning
What questions can I ask?
What have they learnt?
Do I need to alter the lesson?

Students
Current performance
What do the students know?
What can they do?

Assessment
How does it affect their self-esteem and motivation?

Targets
What next?

Sharing learning objectives
Do they know what to do?
Do they know why they are doing the activities?

Recording
What can remain stored in my head?
What do I need to record?

What do I need to report to the students?

Reporting
Who needs to know (students, parents, other teachers)?
What form of report?

Self- and peer assessment
How well am I doing?
How can I improve?
What can I learn from others?

Feedback to students
How can I tell them to improve?
What form will feedback take (written, oral, comment, grade)?

Assessment of learning (summative)
What is their current performance?

Assessment of learning (formative)
How could they improve?
How can they close or bridge the gap?

Teacher assessment
What is the purpose of the assessment? What form will it take?
What do they know and understand? What can they do?
Is the assessment valid, reliable and manageable?

Figure 2.1
(reproduced by kind permission of RoutledgeFalmer)

Planning for classroom-based assessment

What are the mechanisms associated with establishing meaningful assessment in the classroom? Any classroom-based activity should obviously be planned by the teacher before the lesson starts; planning for assessment is no different. Lesson planning should begin with a consideration of what the students *already* know, understand and are capable of doing; what you *want* them to know, understand and do as a consequence of the lesson; and how you will *measure* this change. All of these are essentially 'assessment-driven' considerations.

Weeden *et al.* (2002) summarize the processes and purposes of assessment in the diagram opposite (see Figure 2.1). Here we see how planning assessment activities raises questions – not only about learning objectives and student tasks, but also about when and where assessment opportunities might present themselves. How could these help us to ascertain students' learning? The teaching and learning activities should lead the teacher into considering how he or she could assess the students' learning and whether this will be predominantly summative ('What is their current performance?'), or formative ('How could they improve?'). There is also the important issue of whether the assessment methods are valid, reliable and fit for purpose (see Chapter 4). The 'cycle' is completed by considerations of monitoring, evaluation, recording and reporting.

It is not by chance that students are placed at the centre of Figure 2.1. The formative purposes of assessment are clearly stressed within the diagram, which intentionally locates students as the focus for the assessment process, with any information gathered being used to feedback (or feedforward) to enhance student learning.

Immediately before teaching a lesson it is worthwhile quickly reconsidering where assessment opportunities should arise. Most lesson plans, for whichever subject, tend to follow a reasonably common format. This might normally include: lesson (learning) aims and objectives; skills; methods/procedures: starter, main activities (student/teacher), plenary; homework; differentiation; evaluation. Each of these has an assessment dimension which should ideally be considered during the planning stage, just before teaching, in the lesson itself and reflectively afterwards.

For example, the range of assessment considerations within a typical lesson plan might be as broad as follows:

◆ *Lesson (learning) aims and objectives*
What are the educational intentions of this lesson? Will the context be clear to students? How can I assess this? What should I ask/get students to do to ensure the lesson encourages new learning? Are my 'starting points' right? Will the students be able to engage with the lesson? Am I clear about the learning objectives? Will the students be clear about what they have to do?

◆ *Skills*
Am I introducing new skills? Or building on ones already learnt? Do I know what the students can already do? What will I need to do to assess student competence in these skills?

◆ *Methods/ procedures: starter, main activities (student/teacher), plenary*
What will I expect students to recall from previous lessons? How will I introduce new concepts/content/ideas/skills? How will I assess what they know, understand and can do? What is implied by the learning objectives? What needs emphasis? What can be assumed? How will I recognize, measure and assess learning?

◆ *Homework*
What is the best way to 'continue' this lesson? What are appropriate assessment tasks for students to complete without my direct support?

◆ *Differentiation*
Who will need help? In what form? To do what? Which parts of the lesson will be difficult for all/some of the students? How will I know? How/when should I intervene?

◆ *Evaluation*
Did we meet the lesson/learning objectives? How can this be assessed accurately? What is the next step – for me (as teacher), for the students (as learners), for specific students (differentiation)? What targets now need to be set? What will I give the students as feedback? How is it best to give this? What do I wish to record as achievement? Did the students understand *how* they were learning as well as *what* they learnt? (After Butt 2002)

When planning, it is best to think about lessons from the perspective of the student. In assessment terms this requires a consideration of where students should 'be' when they have completed each lesson (Butt 2006b). It is worthwhile using the following prompts as they focus on what students should know, understand and be able to do:

- **Know that** . . . (Knowledge: factual information, for example, names, places, symbols, formulae, events).
- **Be able to** . . . (Skills: using knowledge, applying techniques, analysing information, etc.).
- **Understand how/why** . . . (Understanding: concepts, reasons, effects, principles, processes, etc.).
- **Be aware of** . . . (Attitudes and values: empathy, caring, sensitivity towards social issues, feelings, moral issues, etc.). (DfES/ QCA 2002, p. 72)

The ways in which these are assessed will be up to the teacher. But lessons must not just assess what is easiest to assess. This implies that lessons should not always cover the same 'assessment ground', for if we regularly use just one or two assessment methods and techniques we tend to receive similar assessment information (Butt 2006b).

Conclusions

This chapter started by posing the important question of how theory can inform practice, specifically within the field of educational assessment. It has demonstrated that knowledge of both learning and assessment theory, coupled with practical experience in the classroom, can provide a powerful means of improving student experience. We not only need to know *what* works – which can be gleaned from trial and error, consulting more experienced professionals and reading education texts – but also (and more importantly) *why* it works. Furnished with this information we can better understand how to react to new challenges by taking action informed by theory.

The ways in which assessment can be used to promote learning, the connections between social constructivist learning theory and assessment, and the importance of assessment planning show how assessment can help to improve students' attainment. However, we also need to apply some caveats: to create and implement an effective formative assessment strategy takes time and effort, both on the part of the teacher *and* the learner. The most significant changes often have to come from the student, who may have lost motivation as a consequence of enduring years of failure reinforced by poorly executed summative assessment. Day-to-day assessment should be focused on the needs of the learner. Each student should feel secure that success is a realistic expectation and that their teacher/assessor is willing to support them in achieving their goals. All learners can achieve something and should be given the opportunities to show what they know, understand and can do. It is worth remembering that continued failure is hugely de-motivational, particularly for low attainers whose achievements may need to be carefully 'scaffolded' and encouraged.

Formative assessment is all about helping students to improve their assessed performance as a result of achieving success in their learning. It is the act of 'closing the gap' between their current performance and realistic expectations of what they can achieve in the future. This implies clear planning and communication on the part of the teacher, coupled with engagement and effort on the part of the student.

3 | Can assessment raise standards?

Education is currently immersed in a standards culture, or, more accurately, a need to both meet and then raise standards. But what are educational standards? Do they refer solely to student achievement and attainment, or are they primarily a measure of teacher and school performance? (Butt and Smith 1998). Standards can loosely be described as agreed levels of performance or quality, which should ideally be devised by professionals within a particular field rather than being imposed on them by others. In education, the 'standards debate' has tended to focus on the publication of assessment data – a legal requirement for schools since the 1990s. In England and Wales the construction of league tables of schools' performance based on their annual GCSE, AS and A level results has increased the national monitoring and accountability of schools and LAs. These league tables can then be used as a crude means of determining the standard at which any particular school is performing. Public examination results are central to the government's rhetoric on educational standards: schools that record high percentages of students achieving five 'good' GCSEs (usually considered as GCSE grades A* to C) are deemed to be of high quality; by contrast, schools of a lower standard (those which have below 30 per cent of students at these grades, now called National Challenge Schools) become the focus of various initiatives pressurizing them to restructure, or close.

Examination results are therefore used to determine minimum standards of performance, create competition and (in theory) drive up standards. The conversion of 'failing' schools into Academies is a good example of how assessment evidence is used as a trigger to initiate change. However, using examination data is not the only, or indeed often the most appropriate, means of determining educational standards in schools. Many teachers would argue that the measurement of educational quality should also consider *inter alia* the development of the whole child, rather than just a narrow analysis of summative assessment data. Unfortunately, attempting to measure standards in this way proves to be challenging, costly and time consuming – it can also be as subjective as using real grade scores. The dilemma is that although equating educational standards to examination performance is limiting and dangerous, it currently appears to be the most workable, economic and transferable way of determining national standards in schools. Inspection reports from the Office for Standards in Education (OfSTED) are also used in concert with assessment data to evaluate school performance, but the latter remains the main foundation for comparing standards between institutions.

Almost every phase of education, from nursery schools and kindergartens to higher education institutions, is now measured against some form of standards. This has tended to have a centralizing, bureaucratic and controlling effect on educational practice – where standards become narrowly equated with performance management and the achievement of set targets. Interestingly, Mary Jane Drummond (2008) informs us that many years ago a paragraph in the Hadow Report on Infant and Nursery Schools (Board of Education 1933) took a very direct stance *against* the use of standards to measure the educational experience of young children when it stated 'a uniform standard to be reached by all children (should not) be expected. The infant school has no business with uniform standards of attainment' (para. 105). Indeed, Drummond (2008) believes that children's work is 'unique, unpredictable, (and) magnificent' (p. 10), and that no standards can routinely be applied to measure student achievement. Standards are also applied to the performance of the professionals who work in education. Trainees undergoing Initial Teacher Training (ITT), Newly Qualified Teachers (NQTs) in their induction period, teachers who aspire to achieve Advanced Skills Teacher (AST) status, and even Teaching Assistants (TAs) and Higher Level Teaching Assistants (HLTAs) all have sets of standards which they must meet. Therefore, not only the attainment of children, but also the performance of education professionals, is imbued with the standards culture – even though many would challenge the standards imposed upon them and the mechanisms by which these are used to 'drive up' quality and performance.

Schools are not the only riders on the standards carousel. The language of performance and achievement, couched in terms of 'standards', is commonly used throughout the public sector. There is no universal agreement about what constitutes acceptable standards, even though this term is widely used in educational circles and is common in newspapers and the media. It would be enlightening to consider the standards that education professionals would ascribe to themselves – what *they* see as significant in their professional lives – and to compare these with the standards imposed by others. Essentially, different standards will reflect what different groups value. Unfortunately the 'top down' approach to establishing standards adopted by governments has tended to demonize teachers as the cause of many educational problems, rather than considering them as a source of solutions. The effect has been to both alienate and disillusion teachers.

The 'standards debate' routinely focuses on whether educational standards are rising or falling in England and Wales, particularly when public examination results are released each August. National newspapers regularly report that students have achieved another 'record year', with higher proportions passing their examinations and gaining better grades than previously. This is inevitably accompanied by claims that standards must be falling and by reflections on a 'golden age' of public examinations in the 1950s and early 1960s, when standards were higher: the reasoning is that the top grades in GCSE and A level are now 'easier' to achieve, therefore standards *must* be slipping. But statistics which indicate that more students are currently passing examinations at higher grades do not necessarily prove that exams are getting easier, nor that standards are falling. It is important to realize that standards are not maintained (or improved) by adopting the mindset that certain numbers of students must fail to make an exam worthwhile; better to think in terms of wanting to maximize the number who achieve than falsely creating excellence ('high standards') by always being tough on a given percentage who sit an examination. Rigour is essential, but this will not be built on systems that either make young people jump over unrealistic and unnecessary examination hurdles, or casually reward them just for turning up. In this respect the assessment 'numbers game' is revealing. In the 1950s and 1960s comparatively few young people sat O levels (a forerunner, in part, of the GCSE) and A levels, for these were examinations designed for the academic élite. However, over time, the purpose of such examinations has changed – as has the range of candidates who sit them. Arguably this is reflected by the rising percentages of young people who have entered higher education during the post-war period, students who have largely used the academic qualifications they gained at school as their means of accessing undergraduate courses. For example, in 1960 only some 9 per cent of the 18- to 19-year-old population entered higher education (27 per cent of the 'non-manual background' cohort, and only 4 per cent of the 'manual background' cohort, in this age range). In 1980 this had risen to 12 per cent entering higher education (33 per cent non-manual, 7 per cent manual), while in 2007 the figure was 40 per cent (50 per cent non-manual, 22 per cent manual) (see Gorard *et al.* 2007). Today the government has an aspiration that around 50 per cent of young people will enter higher education, with the majority of students 'staying on' in schools after they reach the statutory leaving age. Examination results still provide the rather crude 'sheep and goats' division between those who can progress up the educational ladder and those who have to step off – but different educational programmes and forms of assessment now offer a much wider range of experiences, skills and competencies to young people. Combined with vocational qualifications and the rise of Diplomas, the whole purpose of public examinations has broadened, both in terms of the methods of assessment and the content covered. Any attempt at comparing examination questions and scripts with those that existed 50 years ago, in an effort to gauge whether standards are changing, is therefore largely futile – even in relatively 'pure' subjects such as Mathematics. Certainly what is taught and examined in the social sciences has moved on dramatically, such that the performance of students from as little as ten years ago will bear few valid comparisons to those of the present day. Examinations, both at GCSE and A level, are not now intended for a small élite that will progress to university, while many of the skills that were previously deemed important for candidates to possess, such as knowledge recall and memorization, are becoming more redundant in this computer-dominated age.

League tables

Using single pieces of data, such as raw examination scores, to create league tables of school performance has proved problematic. Crude applications of such data, which imply that educational quality can easily be judged on very limited information, should be resisted.

Detailed performance indicators exist that can arguably provide more rounded appreciations of standards, but these tend to require significantly higher inputs of time, effort and finance to construct. League tables tend to skew educational processes – they force teachers and students to concentrate on aspects of education that do not necessarily support learning, but might raise the performance of those who sit on particular grade boundaries. For example, the award of a grade C or above at GCSE is still seen by many (including the government) as a 'pass' – despite the fact that all the grades, from A* to G, are passes, with each indicating a different level of achievement. Grade C, therefore, only crudely represents the division between high and low achievers, with those who gain more than five GCSEs above grade C performing at the nationally acceptable standard. The effect of using assessment data in this way is that most schools concentrate their efforts on raising the performance of their potential D grade students to a C, thus maximizing their standing in the league tables. By targeting effort and resource in this way, those students who are 'more able' or 'less able' will potentially receive less teacher attention. Many teachers would wish to celebrate the significance of a child raising his or her predicted performance from (say) a grade F to a D as an illustration of good educational achievement, for this may reveal more about the standards of education in a school than the award of an A* grade to a more able student.

An unfortunate consequence of using league tables has been an increase in 'game playing' by certain schools keen to improve their position. Before measures were taken by the government in 2006 to stop such practices – by making performance in English and Maths GCSEs central to overall school performance – some schools used equivalence tariffs between academic and vocational qualifications as a means of artificially boosting their apparent performance. In the late 1990s, when parity of esteem between academic and vocational qualifications was being strongly pursued, some schools entered large numbers of students for (intermediate) General National Vocational Qualifications (GNVQs) – where each pass 'scored' the equivalent of four grade C GCSEs. By entering candidates for a GNVQ, these schools only needed students to achieve a grade C in one other GCSE to reach the benchmark of 'five GCSEs above grade C'. Schools that had previously languished far down the examination league tables suddenly found themselves celebrated among the nation's most improved institutions.

'Value added'

Stephen Gorard (2001, 2002, 2005, 2008) has written extensively on the problems associated with trying to determine the 'value added' by schools in raising student attainment. He argues that when we examine the claims for how effective one school is compared to another in adding value, there is little discernible difference in improvements in student performance between schools who teach similar groups of learners. That is, in schools with broadly 'equivalent' student cohorts, variations in teaching appear to have only very limited influence on the value added to student performance. There are also major difficulties in trying to correlate assessment data collected on students early in their school careers with their later performance scores. As such, Gorard (2008) believes that many claims for identifying value added, based on single sampling methods, are deeply flawed.

Value added calculations used by the DCSF (and DfES before them) have always been controversial (see Schagen 2006). Indeed, value added scores may actually tell us very little, either about the performance of particular schools or about how different schools compare to each other. Making the analysis more complex by adding extra factors seems to have little effect, other than improving the observation of 'performance' in some areas (such as attainment) at the expense of evaluating performance in others (such as dropout) (see Gorard 2008). Thus:

> Until concerns about value added analysis have been resolved, it is not reasonable to use them for practical purposes. Parents cannot rely on them when choosing schools. School leaders cannot rely on them to judge the effectiveness of teachers or departments, and officials cannot rely on them to make decisions about the quality of education delivered in schools. (Gorard 2008, p. 184)

Year-on-year improvements in grade scores and pass rates may not tell us whether students are learning better, or teachers teaching better. Trends in such data reveal nothing particularly significant about improvements in standards, but simply indicate that students are getting better drilled and prepared for taking exams. Annually improving pass rates, Gorard would argue, simply reflect better performance at test-taking rather than any evidence of better learning.

Although assessment evidence is increasingly used by governments as a means of supporting policy implementation and of checking whether such policies are broadly successful, using assessment data in this way unearths a number of validity issues and unrealistic assumptions about what such data can legitimately tell us. The main concerns are whether assessment data is capable of accurately and objectively measuring individual performance and attainment; whether common standards exist that can be sensibly measured; whether schools and teachers can have their performance assessed through league tables and value added; whether externally set performance indicators are accurate; and whether 'naming and shaming' failing institutions ultimately raises standards. At the heart of these concerns is the belief that assessment should not just be about the measurement, but the improvement, of learning. As Gorard (2010), notes,

> In England all schools are annually required to provide figures for the National Pupil Database (NPD) and the Pupil-Level Annual School Census (PLASC). Both databases ostensibly have records for all pupils at school in England (but necessarily excludes any pupils not registered). A glimpse of the importance of missing data is revealed by the fact that in some years around 10 per cent of the individual pupil records are un-matched across the two databases.

Testing has a significant impact on teaching and learning. Unfortunately the positive benefits, in terms of instrumental improvement in grades, may be short term. Changing classroom practice to focus students on how to achieve better performance in examinations usually has an immediate, positive impact – increased percentages achieving higher grades – but this may only last for two or three years before performance plateaus. The effect on other aspects of students' educational experience (enjoyment, engagement, motivation to learn) may be negative, while standards of teaching may not have improved. A further characteristic of high stakes testing – grade inflation – provides more cause for concern. Grade inflation is the inexorable, if gradual, increase in the number of students who achieve the highest grades; this obviously again calls into question the whole use of league tables to measure changes in standards. The reliability and validity of using high stakes assessment scores and aspirational targets in this way seems doubtful if grades simply 'drift' upwards annually. Similarly, inflated grading of students during earlier Key Stages means that when they are more accurately assessed later on, they can hope to show only very modest improvements, which in itself is de-motivational and educationally damaging.

Accountability

The connections between accountability and assessment are strong; indeed we have seen how assessment evidence in the form of league tables of examination results, or other assessment scores, are regularly used to hold the performance of students, teachers, headteachers, schools and LAs to account. The constant pressure to perform better, often measured by monitoring the percentages of students who achieve particular grades in public examinations or levels in National Curriculum SAT/teacher assessments, has both a positive and a negative impact on teaching and learning. The consequences of failing to meet particular targets created from these 'key indicators' can be painful – ultimately, in the most extreme cases, leading to inspections, removal of senior managers, school closures and loss of jobs. The accountability lexicon that surrounds all this – schools receiving 'notice to change', being subject to 'special measures', or whose status is 'at risk' – is now commonly understood.

Schools receive their fair share of 'carrot and stick' as a consequence of the application of accountability measures. The intention of fostering accountability in British schools is to judge how effective they (and the components that constitute them) are at 'delivering' education. But using raw examination scores to determine schools 'at risk' is crude, while the measures used to effect change may have positive impacts in some areas (raising exam scores), but negative impacts in others (raising student dissatisfaction, increasing truancy, greater teacher stress). However, policy-makers welcome the fact that high stakes assessments can have very direct and immediate impacts on practice, particularly when linked to regularly applied accountability systems such as league/performance tables and aggregated examination results. The intentions and consequences are very clear.

Using assessment results as a means of establishing accountability in education is therefore controversial. Governments tend to assume that teachers will be slow and inefficient in implementing change;

therefore accountability systems are used to instil immediacy in the setting of targets and the stimulation of action. Here the language of 'raising standards', 'meeting targets', and 'no child left behind' is heard from policy-makers and ministers in advanced economies when they are impatient to impose change. The consequences of always striving to improve, as measured against key accountability indicators, can have both wanted and unwanted effects: undoubtedly in many schools the pressure to constantly improve has had some positive impacts on student performance, not least because teachers are encouraged to believe that all students can advance and that their performance can positively change. By raising the expectations of student performance, neither the students themselves, nor their schools, are allowed to 'coast'. Once constant improvement becomes an expectation, numerous things happen – management teams prioritize the raising of grades, teachers are encouraged to 'work smarter, not harder' in an effort to improve efficiency, the focus for education becomes the examination – all these changes are designed to maximize performance in examination results. The consequence of such accountability may be shifts in teaching methods and increased 'test practice', prioritization of resources for particular 'indicator' subjects, increased focus on exam performance, and various 'game playing', not all of which may be positive for students' educational experiences. Unfortunately, short-term improvements in examination grades are also subject to the law of diminishing returns, whereby after a particular point increased teacher and student effort has rather negligible impact on grades achieved.

Conclusions

As Stobart (2008) reminds us:

> A key purpose of assessment, particularly in education, has been to establish and raise standards of learning. This is now a virtually universal belief – it is hard to find a country that is not using the rhetoric of needing assessment to raise standards in response to the challenges of globalisation. (p. 24)

Testing regularly receives a 'bad press', with high stakes summative assessment often demonized for its negative impact on teaching and learning. This may be unfair. However, it is very apparent, as discussed in this chapter, that the narrow use of assessment data for accountability purposes is problematic. Where national league tables have been removed, as in Wales and Scotland, accountability by examination scores has been replaced by the use of local teacher assessments – resulting in interesting changes in classroom practice. National educational standards cannot be judged simply on pass rates. But we must be honest in acknowledging that we currently could not run our education system *without* testing – for our certification, awarding and selection processes all rely on it. Those who question whether high stakes testing is required at all, in the belief that the removal of such tests would improve the quality of education in schools, may need to ponder on whether the impact of so doing would be entirely positive. There are many teachers for whom the existence of summative tests provides a helpful focus and structure for their teaching. These teachers often manage to balance the need for constructive, engaging pedagogy with the ultimate demands of testing, without recourse to 'teaching to the test'. We obviously need to avoid a situation where:

> Schooling becomes more about gaining the right qualifications than about the learning that these are meant to represent. So learning becomes instrumental and teaching becomes a soulless preparation for the test. (Stobart 2008, p. 114)

In the standards debate it is apparent that improved test scores do not automatically imply improved learning – they may merely reflect improved ability at taking tests. Improvements in learning can almost certainly not be measured through changes in assessed scores. The use of a number of fine-grained indicators (the plural is important here) is needed if an accurate understanding of what constitutes high standards in education is to be achieved.

4 | The influence of 'high stakes' and 'low stakes' assessment

Educational assessment can be divided into two broad categories – 'high stakes' and 'low stakes' assessment. These terms describe the potential impact on students of performing badly, or well, in the different types of assessments. Therefore, 'low stakes' assessments potentially have only a limited impact on a student's future educational, or career, prospects. The term is often loosely applied to most of the day-to-day assessment that occurs in school – such as assessing classroom-based work, oral assessment through question and answer, or short end-of-unit tests. Here students will have numerous opportunities to improve their performance in the future, for the main point of such assessment is the enhancement of their educational progress. By contrast, 'high stakes' assessment usually refers to public examinations and 'one-off' tests that may have longer lasting significance for a student's educational and life journey. The consequences may not be just for the student, for 'accountability may mean it is the teacher, school and education authority – rather than the individual student – for whom the consequences are greatest' (Stobart 2008, p. 20).

Consider the following section from a newspaper article written by Simon Jenkins in which he reflects on some of the impacts of the 'high stakes' assessment 'industry'. In this piece he is not so much concerned with the effects of assessment on the individual student, but wishes to question whether the 'high stakes' external assessment system in Britain is fit for purpose:

> Organising an examination for Britain's teenagers should not be too tough a job. For half a century, local government managed it. Yet from the moment testing was nationalised under the Tories it went berserk. Ministers floundered, claiming to 'need to know' everything about the nation's young. In the decade from its introduction by John Patten in 1993, the cost of testing and

league tables rose from £10m to £610m. Each July saw a flood of 'exam fiasco' stories. Nobody could agree over standards. A secretary of state – Estelle Morris – resigned, and officials and private companies came, went, resigned or were sacked.

Last summer the testing regime reached its nadir. Nobody had been found in all Britain up to the task of running an attainment test for 14-year-olds. The 'market price' for such a paragon was eventually fixed at a salary of £328,000, a flat in west London, membership of a yacht club in Sydney harbour and six club-class tickets round the world. This obscene reward went to an Australian, Ken Boston, who proved unable to do the job without spending a further £156m on an American company, ETS (Educational Testing Services). In July hundreds of thousands of exam papers were delayed or improperly marked, and another fiasco was declared as such by Lord Sutherland in his SATs inquiry report last night. (Jenkins 2008)

We should not lose sight of this perspective, for any discussion of the effects of 'high stakes' testing should not only identify the positives and negatives for students, but also consider whether our approach to assessment is appropriate at the national scale.

The implications of doing well, or badly, in 'high stakes' assessments can be considerable, because their results affect the future pathways available to students. In essence, the outcome of such tests can determine:

♦ The next stage of a student's learning.
♦ The choice of educational courses and qualifications available.
♦ Acceptance by a particular academic institution.
♦ Employment prospects. (Butt 2005b)

As discussed in Chapter 3, at the national scale the results of 'high stakes' assessments can be constructed into league tables, which enable crude measures to be made of the performance of different schools, subject departments, teachers and students. Many teachers are therefore tempted to 'teach to the test' to improve their students' chances of performing well in external examinations – even though they realize that this may have a strong, negative impact on the depth of student learning. The effects of assessment-led teaching are that the educational experience of students can be narrowed to pre-examination 'cramming', question spotting and rote learning – each of which can reduce the enjoyment of the teaching and learning experience. Unfortunately the results of summative assessment can be unreliable in accurately assessing what students know, understand and can do. Setting valid and reliable tasks to obtain an accurate assessment of each student's capabilities and attainment is always difficult, particularly so if we wish to assess, for example, two years' work in a one-and-a-half hour written test. Summative assessments can only ever hope to *sample* the attainment of students and are prone to factors such as student nervousness or illness which can dramatically affect performance. But because 'high stakes', external testing is often regarded as a more objective, valid and rigorous form of assessment than teacher assessment, many teachers narrow their classroom assessment methods to mirror those of 'high stakes' testing. This merely exacerbates and extends the problems of summative assessment. When over-used, summative assessment techniques can be damaging to students, particularly those who regularly perform poorly.

By contrast, 'low stakes' assessments, which are used day-to-day to formatively assess student progress, are generally considered to be more supportive to the process of teaching and learning. They tend to create a stronger, more meaningful educational bond between student and teacher, and may even involve other stakeholders (parents/guardians, teaching assistants, other teachers) in the child's learning. Typically, 'low stakes', classroom-based assessments tend to be short and can be marked quickly, enabling rapid feedback. The use of short, regular assessments in this way, accompanied by constructive feedback from the teacher, can contribute positively to a broad assessment picture being gradually built up on each student.

The effects of an assessment-driven curriculum

Lessons that are too narrowly assessment driven, such as those that feature numerous tests or 'drill and practice' in preparation for 'high stakes' assessment, usually contain fewer classroom discussions and open-ended learning activities. They also tend to reduce the amount of activity-based learning: such as games, role plays, practicals and simulations (Butt 2005b). The reification of summative assessment can also lead to students learning facts and case studies by rote –

usually facilitated by the over-provision of photocopied sheets by teachers. The effect is that although the teacher may feel secure, in that he or she is providing the students with the necessary content to 'deliver' the syllabus or curriculum, the learners do not enjoy the experience and become stressed, overwhelmed and unenthusiastic. This can lead to a 'diminishing return': the teacher may introduce more and more educational material, but the outcome is certainly not greater learning!

By contrast, daily 'low stakes' assessment tends to be more supportive of students' learning. Such assessment favours the use of oral question-and-answer, the observation of students as they work, and the use of self- and peer assessment (Butt 2005b). Teachers will routinely comment on what students are doing in response to assessment tasks, discussing common misconceptions and errors, and setting targets using assessment evidence. These processes are largely educational and formative; hence their inclusion in descriptions of the practice of formative assessment and assessment for learning. Statistically, the amount of 'low stakes', formative assessment that each student experiences during his or her school career will almost certainly be much higher than their involvement in infrequent, 'high stakes', summative testing. It has become fashionable to criticize summative testing – and there are certainly valid reasons for many of these criticisms – but in Chapter 3 it was noted that the British education system could not function without it. 'High stakes' testing currently serves essential certification and selection functions which we would find hard to replicate; if such tests are unpopular or unfit for purpose we have to find other, better, and hopefully less expensive means of delivering these functions. As such, Jenkins' (2008) observations, at the start of this chapter, may have relevance but arguably provide few suggestions for ways forward. It is also important to realize that any form of assessment, whether it be summative or formative, can be performed either well, or badly. Importantly, whatever means of assessment is used it must be valid, reliable and fit for purpose – with that purpose being clear to both assessor and assessed.

The effects of 'high stakes' testing on so-called 'less able' students can be particularly damaging. It is one thing for a student to perform badly in an assessment due to a lack of application and preparation, but quite another due to an innate, (supposedly) unmovable lack of ability. In the first case, greater effort will improve performance, in the second – if one holds a view that intelligence cannot be developed – nothing will make a difference. If ability testing is favoured, those who possess higher abilities will always be at an advantage. This argument underlines all that is wrong with ability testing, which gives the message that those who 'fail' are destined for a life of non-achievement. This negative labelling, sense of failure and inability to improve has a devastating effect on many young people's confidence in their ability to achieve. Only those who believe that their efforts can have a positive impact on their achievement, rather than accepting that their ability was fixed at birth, will progress.

Norm- and criterion-referenced assessment

In 'high stakes' assessment there are two main ways of differentiating between, and ultimately grading, student performance within a population. These are referred to as norm-referenced and criterion-referenced assessment (Glaser 1963).

Norm-referencing involves each student's achievements being compared to those of the rest of the class, year group, or national cohort (Butt 2005b). This follows the principle that the frequency of the marks which a population of students achieves, when displayed on a graph, will approximate to a normal, or bell-shaped, distribution. On such a graph we can determine individual student performance against that of their peers, to see where their marks place them. This form of measuring performance is deeply embedded within our education and assessment culture – enabling teachers to rank order each student's performance against their peers. Whenever there is a need to compare one student's performance with that of others, for certification reasons or to select a fixed number of students to 'pass', then such norm-referenced assessment can be used. In practical terms it is the basis of all 'high stakes' assessment systems such as national tests for SATs, GCSEs, AS and A levels, as well as degree qualifications, although some criterion-referencing is also employed. At the start of the assessment process there are no pre-determined marks against which grades will be awarded to students, although when assessment of this type is carried out annually on a national scale, assessors usually have a good idea of where grade boundaries will fall. So it would initially be impossible to state that a mark of, for example, 60 per cent, would automatically mean that a student would be awarded a grade A. The awarding of grades depends on the performance of the whole population of students taking the test in a particular year. Thus, if the test was very difficult, the range of marks might be quite low with few candidates being awarded top marks – it might be the case that in this year any student who achieved a mark of, for example, 45 per cent or above would be awarded a grade A. If the test was 'easy', it might mean that the boundary for the award of an A grade was as high as 70 per cent.

However, it is possible to pre-determine the percentage, or number, of students you wish to be awarded each grade in a norm-referenced system. You might want to decide beforehand that in an examination that will award grades from A to E (five grades), that the top 10 per cent of marks will be awarded an A, and the bottom 10 per cent an E. This then allows you to step the grades B, C and D in cohorts of the intervening 20 per cent, 40 per cent and 20 per cent of marks between the top and bottom grades (Butt 2005b). Obviously the shape of the normal distribution of marks awarded – whether it appears 'broad and fairly flat' or 'tall and quite thin' (the degree of kurtosis), or whether it is skewed – will determine whether some students achieving a few more marks will make little or no difference to their gaining a particular grade, or whether these few marks mean that numerous candidates fall into a much higher or lower grade band. In most tests, if the number of students assessed is large enough, the distribution of marks will tend to describe a fairly regular normal (bell-shaped) curve. Therefore, as previously suggested, in any external examination set on a national scale where the candidate numbers are large, it is statistically probable that each year group's performance will be very similar. Hence awarding bodies (formerly known as exam boards) and the government can be reasonably confident that the marks for each grade boundary will be similar year on year. Certain statistical limits are placed on where these boundaries are allowed to move each year to ensure that candidate performance does not shift radically.

By contrast, a criterion-referenced system starts from the principle that the nature of student performance needed to achieve a particular grade (or level) can be determined before he or she sits an examination. Here performance standards are already known and fixed before the assessment is taken (Butt 2005b). Written statements of performance, the criteria, are produced such that if a candidate's assessed performance matches the attainment criterion he or she will be awarded the grade associated with it. These criteria (or level descriptions in the National Curriculum) describe what a typical candidate knows, understands and can do if he or she is to fall within this grade/level category. It therefore does not matter how other students perform – any number of students in a particular year can be awarded a particular criterion/level/grade if they meet the standards expressed in the criterion statement. This is different from norm-referenced assessment where each student's performance is compared to that of his or her peers. Traditionally many vocational courses have been assessed against criteria (or 'competences'). Perhaps the most well-known example of such a criterion-based assessment is the practical driving test. Here a pre-determined set of procedures must be carried out competently for the examiner to award a 'pass', regardless of how many other people have already passed that day.

There are two major problems with criterion-based assessment:

1. Accurately and completely describing the criteria necessary to achieve each grade/level beforehand.
2. Judging whether a particular candidate matches completely, or 'best fits', these stated criteria.

Writing criteria that capture the nature of what is to be assessed and what will subsequently be recognized as 'attainment' is never straightforward. Such criteria tend to be written as a hierarchy of statements, with each statement building progressively on the last in 'steps of difficulty', becoming more demanding with each step. Criteria should be understood by both teachers and learners – often there is a problem with regard to the latter, meaning that teachers have regularly re-written criteria in 'student speak' to enable them to more fully understand the levels of performance expected of them. The National Curriculum Level Descriptions (LDs) are a good example of criteria within a (partly) criterion-referenced assessment system (those remaining SATs representing the norm-referenced element of assessment). Some National Curriculum subjects, such as Geography and History, have always been assessed by teachers against the LDs, with no SATs involved in the assessment of student performance – an example of a teacher-assessed criterion-referenced assessment system, applied on a national scale. The assessment of the National Curriculum has developed significantly since its inception through the 1998 Education Reform Act and the subsequent establishment of a Task Group on Assessment and Testing (TGAT) which devised the national assessment system that would accompany it. The initial problem faced by subject working groups who devised both the curriculum for each subject and the criteria for its assessment, was that they attempted to make the criteria do too much. That is, they were tempted to fine-tune the criteria/levels to such a degree that they became very complex, atomized statements of attainment – in some cases becoming an overly elaborate collection of performance statements, in others a mismatch of highly definitive statements and rather broad, over-arching expectations. These naturally became difficult to understand and to apply fairly, and were revised in 1995 following a review by Sir (later Lord) Ron Dearing. The problem with National Curriculum levels/criteria is that they have to provide very broad definitions which encapsulate student learning, which will typically be rewarded with a change of level over two years. Here students are assessed against which level they 'best fit' – an indication of their broad abilities, skills and aptitudes – rather than attempting to achieve a precise understanding of what they specifically know, understand and can do. This may give us a better indication of performance than an examination grade, because we can reflect on the criteria which outline the overall nature of performance required to achieve a level. However, saying, for example, that two students have been assessed by their teacher at level 5 in the Citizenship National Curriculum still gives us no specific indication of what that achievement looks like, of what they have grasped within that level. They may each know, understand and be able to do somewhat different things – some of them similar, some very different – but they may both 'best fit' this particular level. Only if the levels were achieved by having to perform on all aspects of the level criteria would there be close correspondence between the two students. As an indication of what has been learnt, this situation is somewhat better than considering two students who took a summative test and scored the same marks – because these marks may have been gained on different questions which test different things. But there are still uncertainties about what the levels indicate about student learning.

To ensure that assessment processes are valid, reliable and fit for purpose, the two ways of referencing assessment can be used in tandem. However, it is worth remembering that norm-referenced assessment systems only consider the attainments that a population of students actually demonstrates when assessed, they do not seek to match this student performance against previously devised level or criteria statements (of what they 'know, understand and can do'). Although norm- and criterion-referenced assessment are the 'big two' means of measuring student performance, a third method exists: ipsative assessment. Here individual student performance is specifically measured against their previous performance on similar tasks. This form of assessment is particularly helpful in terms of target setting and target getting. In conclusion, Dudley and Swaffield (2008) state in relation to norm-referenced, criterion-referenced and ipsative assessment:

> All assessment involves making judgements in relation to something. For example, we may assess a piece of work by comparing it with that of other students, or with success criteria, or with work of a similar nature produced by the same student. (p. 107)

Validity

The term 'validity' refers to whether a form of assessment actually measures what it claims to measure. Angoff (1988) and Wiliam (2008) both consider that validity is 'an evolving concept', pointing out that one cannot always validate a means of assessment according to what it contains, but only by what it can predict. Wiliam uses the 11+ selection examination for grammar schools as an example of a test which is used because of its *predictive* validity – that is, a test that can successfully predict that those who pass it will 'do well' in the future from receiving a grammar school education. Here the 11+ examination, a test of general intelligence, correlates well with grades achieved in GCSEs five years later – with a figure of 0.7 for this correlation. (By contrast, Wiliam points out that the predictive validity of A level grades to the eventual degree class which students gain at British universities is much poorer, at around 0.3 to 0.4). *Concurrent* validity – using one test to predict performance on another test taken at the same time – is a concept that can also be applied to students' assessed performance.

Validity is a slippery concept because what might be a valid test for one group of students may be less so for another. Wiliam (2008) illustrates this with reference to a history test which also has a high demand in terms of reading ability – therefore for 'more able' students who have good literacy skills, a poor result probably indicates that they do not know much about the aspects of history being tested; but for 'less able' students with poor literacy they may not know much history, or their poor literacy may be hampering their performance, or both. In the situation where the students may be good historians, but their poor literacy levels are getting in the way, this is an example of a test with poor validity – because the variation in students' scores are not mainly related to their ability in history, but to their literacy levels. Wiliam concludes that validity cannot be a *property* of a test, as there is no such thing as a 'valid test'. Another way of thinking about this is to consider the ways in which we might test someone's ability to ride a bicycle: an assessment of their practical ability of riding a bicycle between two points on a course might be considered to be more valid than getting them to write an essay about how to ride a bike.

Stobart (2008) adds:

> Whether an assessment is valid or not depends not only on how well it measures what is being tested, but also on the interpretations that are put on the results. A well-constructed test becomes invalid if the results are misunderstood or wrong interpretations are made. Many of the abuses of assessment stem from what is read into results, and the consequences of this. (p. 174)

Reliability

Reliability is concerned with the accuracy with which an assessment measures what it purports to measure (Black and Wiliam 2008a). Wiliam (2008) refers to this concept as follows: 'A reliable test is one in which the scores that a student gets on different occasions, or with a slightly different set of questions on the test, or when someone else does the marking, does not change very much' (p. 128). The range of scores for test reliability varies between 1, for a totally reliable test, and 0, for a totally unreliable test. Wiliam (2001) points out that achieving perfection in terms of test reliability is impossible, such that no test can ever claim to have achieved a score of '1'. Interestingly, public examinations such as GCSEs and A levels have a reliability generally assessed in the range 0.75 to 0.85, while teacher-devised tests used in schools generally have a reliability score well below this. Great care must therefore be taken when drawing conclusions from single tests, which may have very limited reliability.

Issues of validity and reliability again confirm that assessment is an art, not a science. It is therefore important that interpretation of the results of assessments is carried out carefully. The bias that is often ascribed to tests is actually related to the *inferences* we draw from test results, which are not qualities of the tests themselves. So, in Geography, if we use a map to test spatial cognition skills, and boys outperform girls, this may be because boys are generally better than girls at using maps (Boardman 1990), rather than because there is a particular bias in the test itself. Bias would be a factor if we used the result of this test to infer that boys are better than girls at Geography – they are not, as witnessed by National Curriculum levels assessments and GCSE and A level results over the past twenty years.

Conclusions

We have already seen, in Chapter 3, how assessment can be used for accountability as well as selection purposes. Here our concern has been more about the nature of how the grade is awarded to the student, rather than any consideration of the specific content learned or the process of learning.

Many students see the gaining of qualifications as the main purpose of their education. This utilitarian view – that education simply provides a means of achieving good examination results, primarily to extend educational and employment choices – tends to downgrade the importance of learning. Learning for its own sake is undervalued; it is just a means to an end, rather than an end in itself. Students therefore begin to see much of their learning, and more specifically the act of assessment, as a process of 'hurdling' – merely jumping barriers to get on a course or gain employment, rather than learning for its intrinsic purposes of stimulation, interest, intellectual advancement, curiosity and enjoyment. This has a number of potentially negative impacts on teaching and learning. The curriculum becomes narrowed to serve the needs of the examination, 'teaching to the test' increases, with a concomitant effect on promoting short-term, 'surface' learning. As examination performance improves, due to teachers and students becoming more instrumental and skilled about achieving the desired grades, selection becomes harder. More students achieving higher grades creates problems for those trying to select students for their next educational course, or for employment. In this situation, qualifications ultimately serve as a 'shorthand' proxy of abilities for employers, and in some cases educational institutions, which are less concerned about the content and skills learned by the student, and more about the passing of a qualification at a particular grade.

Many teachers, and others, have a faith in the external examination system that may be somewhat misplaced. They carry the practice and principles of summative assessment into the classroom in the belief that these are the most valid and reliable ways in which to judge student attainment. The reliance on formal tests has also been strongly influenced by the public availability of external assessment results and the creation of league tables. This may partly explain why teachers still tend to value summative assessment methods compared to the often more educationally worthwhile, but time-consuming, formative approaches (Butt 2005b).

5 | Formative and summative assessment: 'We need to talk'

Formative assessment, often referred to as Assessment for Learning (AfL), has been strongly promoted in the UK over the last decade. Black and Wiliam (2003) remind us that the term 'formative evaluation' was first associated with teaching and curriculum matters in 1967, as used by Michael Scriven (Scriven 1967), while Bloom, Hastings and Madaus gave the term 'formative assessment' its current meaning (Bloom *et al.* 1971). The surge of recent interest in the formative, educational aspects of assessment has been expressed in a number of ways: through government education policy initiatives, such as the promotion of AfL in the Key Stage 3 National Strategy; through the work of assessment groups, such as the Assessment Reform Group (ARG); and through research, which has resulted in an array of academic and professional publications (Gardner 2008, Stobart 2008, Black *et al.* 2003, Black and Wiliam 2008b, Brooks 2002, Dann 2002, Swaffield 2008). As might be expected, not all of these approaches have yielded success – for example, the OfSTED evaluation of the impact of the National Strategies in supporting AfL discovered that 'the impact on achievement and provision was no better than satisfactory in almost two-thirds of the schools visited' (OfSTED 2008, p. 1).

The main purpose of formative assessment is to create a closer link, essentially a *relationship*, between assessment and learning. It focuses on what happens in the classroom, on the nature of interactions between (and among) teachers and learners, and on the quality of their educational experience. As we have seen in Chapter 4, 'high stakes', summative assessment tends to exacerbate a dislocation between assessment and learning. To divorce learning and assessment in this way means that valuable assessment information which could be used to improve students' learning is lost: awarding a grade as the sole measure of what the learner has memorized or understood is essentially a wasteful process. Assessment *for* learning therefore affirms that teachers should make assessment a force for student support, motivation and growth, rather than judgement.

Harlen (2008a) illustrates the key aspects of formative assessment as follows:

◆ Evidence is gathered about ongoing learning activities that can be used to make decisions about how to help further learning.
◆ The evidence is judged in terms of progress towards the detailed lesson goals; these goals may vary for different individual pupils or for groups and so comparisons between pupils are not sensible or justified.
◆ Pupils are aware of their lesson goals and can help in deciding their next steps towards the goals.
◆ The process is cyclical and ongoing, information being gathered and used as an integral part of teaching and learning.
◆ No judgement of grade or level is involved; only the judgement of how to help a student take the next steps in learning, so reliability is not an issue. Information is gathered frequently by teachers who will be able to use feedback to correct any mistaken judgement. (p. 139)

In practice, classroom-based formative assessment:

> . . . can occur many times in every lesson. It can involve several different methods for encouraging students to express what they are thinking and several different ways of acting on such evidence. It has to be within the control of the individual teacher and, for this reason, change in formative assessment practice is an integral and intimate part of a teacher's daily work. (Black *et al.* 2003, p. 2)

The teacher's view of what assessment can do to improve student learning is important. If we feel that assessment is simply a means of measuring (or reaffirming) what children have been genetically pre-determined to achieve, then assessment will serve little educational purpose. However, if we believe that students can improve and grow, and that teachers have agency in helping students achieve this goal, then assessment provides a vehicle for enhancing learning.

The Assessment Reform Group (ARG) outlines ten principles that underpin assessment for learning. The group believes that AfL:

- ◆ is part of effective planning;
- ◆ focuses on how pupils learn;
- ◆ is central to classroom practice;
- ◆ is a key professional skill;
- ◆ is sensitive and constructive;
- ◆ fosters innovation;
- ◆ promotes understanding of goals and criteria;
- ◆ helps learners to know how to improve;
- ◆ develops the capacity for self- (and peer) assessment;
- ◆ recognizes all educational achievement. (Adapted from ARG 2002, cited in Butt 2006b)

When considering the question of why formative assessment should be taken seriously, Black *et al.* (2003) suggest six main reasons: that formative assessment raises the scores of students on conventional tests; that the changes in classroom practice associated can be successfully incorporated in normal classroom work; that such change requires redistribution rather than an increase in effort ('working smarter, not harder'); that stepped change rather than a big 'leap in the dark' is possible; that teachers come to enjoy their work more as changes resonate more closely with their professional values; and that students enjoy, understand and value their learning more.

Hargreaves (2005) raises interesting questions about the concepts of 'assessment for learning', 'assessment' and 'learning'. She believes that the conceptions of 'assessment-as-measurement' and 'learning-as-attaining' objectives are currently dominant among policy-makers, but that educationists should use these categorizations to encourage thinking 'outside the box'; that is, 'to think critically about which approaches to assessment, learning and therefore assessment-for-learning we really value and want to promote for young people' (Hargreaves 2005, p. 214). Recognizing that the 'summative/formative' and 'assessment for learning/assessment of learning' duality has dominated recent debate about assessment, Hargreaves urges that a different conception – that is, of knowledge being fixed and external to the learner, or (co-)constructed by the learner – should drive decisions about the type and purpose of the assessment methods employed.

Assessment careers

As Paul Black and Dylan Wiliam assert, 'It has long been recognised that assessment can support learning as well as measure it' (Black and Wiliam 2003, p. 623). However, the experiences of the learner need to be considered within the context of assessment. We are told that formative assessment strategies can help to motivate learners, enhance educational attainment, promote autonomy and solve problems of under-achievement, but what is the learner's experience? The notion of 'learning careers', 'learning identities' and 'assessment careers', which describe how students develop both ways of learning and dispositions towards education which are particularly affected by assessment methods, are helpful here (Pollard and Filer 1999, Reay and Wiliam 1999, Ecclestone and Pryor 2003). Alongside socio-cultural aspects of assessment (Torrance and Pryor 1998, Filer and Pollard 2000), developing a knowledge of students' relationships with assessment and learning to support formative action is important.

Ecclestone and Pryor (2003) have researched the 'assessment careers' of students from primary school to post-16 education, drawing on factors that impact upon the ways in which young people view their education. These factors, each of which has an effect on students' motivation to learn, include: personal dispositions and learning strategies; reactions to learning institutions and teachers; peer norms; teaching and learning activities; and assessment. The significance of such research is that it looks at the notion of individual assessment systems in forming learning identities, bringing together concepts of 'learning careers' and 'assessment careers'. Ecclestone and Pryor's proposition is that assessment events and practices are especially influential within learning careers. Both summative and formative assessment systems alter the learner's identity and have an effect on their socialization within learning programmes. Indeed, as Filer and Pollard (2000) state, assessment procedures within schools have a profound impact on the self-esteem of children. The learner may see the 'cost' of assessment as being emotional and 'high stakes', closely linked to a risk of failure or of being judged negatively. The students' (and teachers') beliefs about assessment become formed through experience, resulting in some assessment practices becoming accepted and legitimized, while others are rejected.

Importantly, we must acknowledge that much of what AfL claims to deliver may make common sense, but in the main has not been empirically tested. Few empirical studies exist which draw together evidence of the impact of formative assessment on achievement. Additionally, the theoretical foundations for AfL are somewhat modest. As Stobart (2008) states, 'Assessment for Learning is best viewed as an approach to classroom assessment, rather than as a tightly formulated theory' (p. 145). Its popularity with teachers is at least partly related to the fact that it is practical, pragmatic and classroom-based – in itself a dangerous state of affairs if formative assessment becomes reduced to lists of 'tips for teachers' lacking any theoretical underpinning. However, we have seen in Chapter 2 that certain theories of learning are associated with AfL, predominantly within the social constructivist domain.

Summative assessment

Perhaps the best-known forms of summative testing are the 'high stakes', public examinations typified by GCSE and A and AS level testing. Here the assessment processes usually:

> . . . involve tests that are infrequent, isolated from normal teaching and learning, carried out on special occasions with formal rituals, and often conducted by methods over which individual teachers have little or no control. (Black *et al.* 2003, p. 2)

Good summative testing is important to our educational system (see Chapter 4). Our intention should be to use well-designed tests – which are valid, reliable and fit for purpose – to enable an accurate assessment of student attainment. Here the targets that students (and teachers) should aspire to must be clear and supported by the assessment data produced. As a result, appropriate standards should be apparent to teachers and students, commonly understood and nationally agreed. We have seen that assessment information can successfully be used for both educational and bureaucratic purposes – unfortunately, our national assessment system does not currently measure up to these exacting expectations for a number of reasons. The consequences of high stakes, summative testing are therefore generally well known, but not easily remedied:

◆ Summative assessment/testing has developed into a 'high stakes' process, through the use (and abuse) of public examination results. Their importance is huge – to the candidate, the teacher, the school and the government. The high status of examination grades has become a significant influence on policy and practice.

◆ The more important such results have become, the more likely they are to distort the processes they are trying to monitor. Thus, as a means of monitoring teaching and learning, through the proxy of an exam grade, summative tests have distorted what goes on in classrooms. Teachers are tempted to use methods that promote superficial rote-learning to enhance their pupils' exam performance, rather than encouraging deep learning. Schools put more effort into raising achievement on C–D borderlines, or enter pupils for exams that carry a greater tariff, to improve league table results. These actions are not supported by sound educational reasoning.

◆ The more important test results become, the more teachers 'teach to the test'.

◆ In systems where year-on-year performance in exams is monitored and known, with access to past papers and reports on candidate performance, the more fixed the assessment-led curriculum becomes. Experimentation in curriculum design and teaching approaches risks a decline in candidate performance. Awarding bodies therefore tend to dominate the development of the curriculum.

◆ Exam technique is taught, as is question spotting. These do not necessarily improve learning, but may improve performance.

◆ When exam results are the major arbiter of future life and education choices, pupils, employers, parents, educational institutions, and society treats these as the ultimate 'end point' of education, rather than a (flawed) indicator of achievement. (After Madaus 1988)

Harlen (2008a) further illustrates the key aspects of summative assessment as follows:

◆ The process takes place at a particular time, it is not ongoing and not cyclical.

◆ The evidence used relates to the same goals for all pupils.
◆ The evidence is interpreted in terms of publicly available criteria.
◆ The judgement is reported in terms of levels, grades or scores, which need to be underpinned by some quality assurance procedures.
◆ Pupils have a limited role, if any, in the process. (pp. 139–40)

Hence the dominance of national testing and 'high stakes' assessment in education tends to skew classroom practice, and places the assessment *of* learning on a pedestal.

Improving summative testing

Stobart (2008) identifies four practical steps which would help to create better summative testing and ultimately result in more positive effects on teaching and learning:

1. Make explicit the purpose and learning on demand

Reflection on the *aims* of the course/learning unit, rather than the *content*, should determine the purpose and form of its assessment. Problems occur when the aims of the curriculum are largely ignored and assessments are devised almost entirely on what has been taught – a situation which applied to the assessment of the National Curriculum in the early 1990s.

2. Encourage 'principled' knowledge through less predictable questions

Ensure that students have to rely on their understanding to answer questions, rather than being able to succeed through simple recall. This requires examinations to include 'unfamiliar questions', to break away from the tradition of looking at past papers to predict likely questions and to avoid the practice of teachers and students relying on previously prepared answers. This encourages more active, flexible, problem-based teaching and learning which is necessary to cope with such questions. In this situation, the classroom-based assessment will not always have to mimic what is likely to appear in the summative tests – teachers will, by necessity, have to construct questions that push students into new ways of using their knowledge, understanding and skills. In the process of doing so, misconceptions and misunderstandings will be revealed.

3. Keep it as authentic as possible

Make sure that tests reflect the skills desired within the teaching and learning of the curriculum. This is the essence of authenticity in testing – that is, we test what is taught and learnt. Students would therefore have to show that they can actually perform relevant tasks – for example, getting a musician to play a piece of music, a linguist to speak in a foreign language, or a geographer to carry out an enquiry in the field. This creates problems of standardization and manageability, but would make assessment more valid and reliable.

4. Dependability

Ensuring that assessments are authentic partly links to whether assessments are valid and reliable. How dependable an assessment is connects to the balance between validity and reliability (see Chapter 4); if these aspects are appropriately balanced then the assessment will be dependable. Stobart (2008) illustrates this by referring to a multiple-choice test which could be highly reliable in terms of marking, but which might have very little validity if it was attempting to assess reflective writing for example. This test would not be very dependable because of the imbalance between validity and reliability.

Unfortunately, even in schools that have advanced the role of AfL, the techniques associated with formative assessment are often abandoned when high stakes summative assessments appear on the horizon. It seems that the influence of such testing is so strong that formative approaches are rejected immediately prior to examinations, with teachers reverting back to the more practical and 'authentic' exam preparation of 'teaching to the test'.

Communicating assessment – the use of oral question and answer

The next section of this chapter focuses on an important aspect of AfL: the need for teachers not only to use oral assessment correctly, but also to communicate assessment findings with their students. Here I concentrate specifically on classroom-based, oral question and answer; in Chapter 6, I broaden the focus to look at the feedback of assessment information from teacher to learner through dialogue, discussion and written comments.

One of the most common forms of assessment, used on a daily basis by most teachers, is the assessment of students' oral responses to questions. This tends to be very 'low stakes' assessment closely linked to the process of learning, rather than the reporting of achievement. Such assessment is also tied to feedback, for the most common communication that students receive from teachers is related to their responses to oral questions (notwithstanding those children who have behavioural issues, which need to be regularly addressed by teachers in class). Question and answer sessions are therefore closely linked to formative assessment and feedback. As with any good assessment practice, this is best conducted as a dialogue between teacher and student, rather than a series of one-sided statements made by the teacher in a transmission–reception model of instruction. This implies that the oral component of a lesson should not be restricted to teacher-led question and answer, but also involve one-to-one dialogue with students, discussions with groups of students engaged in tasks, as well as whole-class conversations. In this way, students are made aware of what they have learnt, how they are learning and where the educational process is leading them next.

The effectiveness of oral assessment is largely determined by three things: the types of questions asked, the ways in which they are asked, and the manner in which student responses are handled.

Many of the questions that teachers ask are 'low order' questions. These are often the first questions asked in a question and answer session to kickstart the lesson, they may be designed to stimulate the students' recall of their previous learning, and are often answered successfully with just a one-word response. Questions of this type might be: 'What term do we give to the movement of water across the earth's surface?', 'Who was the king or queen who succeeded Henry VIII?', 'What is 6 multiplied by 7?' or 'What is the symbol for copper in the periodic table?'. On the basis that one either knows the answer to such a question or does not, the response time given to students is generally small – this is a significant point, as we will see later when we consider the effective use of 'high order' questions in oral assessment. Such short-answer, instant-recall questions only succeed in generating (or more likely reinforcing) surface learning, focused on remembering key words and stimulating progression from one phase of learning to the next.

To be used effectively, 'high order' questions – sometimes referred to as 'big questions' – will usually require the teacher to wait a little longer for an answer from students. Often such questions need to be 'worked out' – these are not instant response questions that students will immediately either know the answer to or not. By treating response times to all questions the same, teachers may restrict the thinking of their students, forcing them to make snap decisions about the answers they offer, or simply encouraging them to give up. Therefore, if you would normally wait a second (or two) for an answer to a 'low order' question, it may be appropriate to wait for three or four seconds before accepting an answer to a high order question. Teachers must not be in too much of a hurry to accept the first 'hands up' that signal that these students think they've got the answer – allow *other* students the time to think as well. This seems straightforward and obvious, but is something of a skill. It is human nature to reward the first student who responds by requesting their answer; this temptation should be avoided if one wants all the students to engage in thinking about the question. It can become embarrassing and stressful if no one offers an answer. Obviously, if students are allowed to shout out answers, this reduces thinking/response times and generally leads to poor classroom management. Allowing extra response time – even extending this by asking a supplementary, supporting question to guide students' thinking – will draw more students into responding, will mean that students give fuller responses and improve the collective thinking processes. The whole point of asking high order questions is to stimulate students' thinking, encourage them to reason through their answers and to engage them in enquiry. The results of so doing suggest that a greater number of students subsequently respond with more confidence and after deeper thinking. Getting students to listen to, sensibly comment on, and extend the answers of their peers is a bonus.

Encouraging student thinking through oral question and answer is a very skilled process. Here teachers are, in effect, assessing all the time and helping to formatively structure students' responses. For example, in response to a partially correct answer, a teacher might extend thinking by commenting 'That's almost it', or 'Nearly there', or 'Yes, but why?', or 'Great idea. What else might be important here?' Significantly, the teacher does not just accept what the student says, but attempts to extend their thinking into new understandings. Students regularly need to be encouraged to say more. If they expect that the question and answer 'game' is short and sharp, dominated by one word answers, then they will neither extend their answers, nor their thinking. Teacher talk dominates the classroom – by restricting the amount that *we* talk, and by encouraging more student involvement, we will improve the learning environment.

Students make judgements about the teacher's educational intentions from their response to question and answer, as well as from a host of non-verbal cues and messages. Teachers' responses to students' oral answers (and statements) are therefore very important, either helping to nurture or destroy a supportive environment for learning. Consider the following exchange between a teacher and student in a Geography lesson:

Teacher: What term do we give to the central area of big cities?
Student: The CBD.
Teacher: Good, the CBD. What does that stand for?
Student: The Central Business District.
Teacher: Excellent!

Now consider what learning has resulted from this. The teacher has asked two related questions, both of which are closed, and has praised the student for answering correctly. But the responses were quick and the student has merely recalled what she already knew – no new learning has occurred. While there is nothing 'wrong' in this – there is a very definite place for recall in the classroom – this exchange has not really moved anyone's learning forward, although it might be the basis for the next stage of learning. What this exchange has *not* done is give the teacher any indication of what other students know, understand or can do – it is possible, although admittedly unlikely, that this student is the only one in the class who knew the term 'Central Business District'. Teacher feedback has been restricted to an acknowledgement that the answers are right. More importantly, this exchange has not given the teacher any sense of the depth of understanding of the term by this student, or any other. What happens in the CBD? What are its characteristics? Why does it form where it does, in the way that it does? Why do most large Western cities have CBDs that exhibit similar spatial patterns and functions? What are the problems of such land use? These are all open questions that the teacher may lead on to – but often they remain unasked and unanswered, with the teacher assuming that much of this is already understood by students. If the teacher is mostly interested in driving the pace of the lesson, by using short, closed questions, and getting the 'right answer' from students, then very little new learning will occur and modest amounts of assessment information can be gathered. Question and answer must become much more student-centred if learning is to advance; teachers must listen to students' responses to open questions and skilfully direct their questions, activities and exposition to address their students' needs, using the assessment information gathered. In the King's, Medway, Oxfordshire Formative Assessment Project (KMOFAP), where a cohort of teachers from secondary schools in two Local Authorities was encouraged to take formative assessment ideas into the classroom, oral questioning became a focus for their assessment practice. As a result, Black *et al.* (2003) reported that:

> . . . teachers . . . now spend more time on preparing quality questions, have richer student involvement and use incorrect answers from both classwork and homework as discussion points to be taken up by the whole class. Questions are often devised to challenge common misconceptions, to create some conflict that requires discussion, or to explore ambiguity that needs clarification before an accepted answer can be formulated. Students are given time to think and sometimes to discuss their thoughts with peers, and then anyone might be asked to respond. Group responsibility is given a high profile in many of the classrooms so that mistakes can be shared and rectified and answers reached collectively and collaboratively. Students are therefore more ready to offer answers and to attempt difficult aspects, as they know that others will help them if they falter. (pp. 39–40)

Setting up discussion within formative assessment

The very nature of dialogue and discussion means that although teachers can plan these activities, and can have strategies to direct them appropriately to maximize their learning and assessment potential, they cannot fully pre-determine their outcomes. Good teachers, who know their students well, may be able to anticipate the kinds of response that they will receive to different oral activities and also the likely nature of their own interventions and challenges to students' learning. Hodgen and Webb (2008) suggest there are certain generic prompts that can be used to get students engaged in oral work, to consider wider issues, and to generate new ideas:

- Tell me about the problem.
- What do you know about the problem? Can you describe the problem to someone else?
- Have you seen a similar problem like this before?
- What is similar? What is different?
- Do you have a hunch? A conjecture?
- What would happen if . . . ? Is it always true that . . . ?
- How do you know that . . . ? Can you justify . . . ? Can you find a different method?
- Can you explain/improve/add to that explanation?
- What have you found out? What advice would you give to someone else about . . . ?
- What was easy/difficult about this task? (p. 83)

Note that these are all open questions, designed to extend thinking, and direct the *students* to talk, rather than relying on the teacher for the answers.

It is unrealistic to expect students who have little experience of forming arguments orally, or of defending their ideas publicly, to be able to do so without preparation and practice. Hence teachers who try to establish dialogue or discussion often get frustrated by students' first attempts at this – sometimes leading to teachers claiming 'My students aren't good at this', 'They don't get it', or 'They aren't capable of handling discussion work'. What is more likely is that the first few times student-centred discussion is tried, it will be messy and problematic, requiring large amounts of teacher intervention. Often this combines with one or two students dominating the process, making others feel alienated and simply reinforcing their non-involvement in any class-based oral work. More time may be needed for students to think, talk about and prepare answers and responses, work over the ideas of others, ask their own questions. The aim must be to establish a culture in which all students are expected and required to contribute, with their contributions being respected and supported by others. Even short whole-class discussions require certain 'rules of engagement' to be established, understood and respected.

Real learning can result from structured discussion and dialogue. Teachers should try not to over-assess – don't leap in to correct initial mistakes and misconceptions, but encourage students to help themselves through various prompts: 'Why do you think that?', 'What hunch do you have about this?', 'Why is that a good/poor answer?', 'What more do you need to find out?' Do not always expect and work for the 'right answer' – often the process of arriving at a reasonable and defensible answer is more important than achieving a one-word, successful response. The temptation, when question and answer is not going smoothly, is for the teacher to either answer their own question, resort to taking answers only from 'bright' students, or to ask so many supplementary questions that students either get further confused or have no problems in answering a grossly simplified version of the original question set. Students understand this and are sophisticated at playing this assessment game with certain teachers. They know that apathetic resistance to questions will eventually mean they will be let off thinking about the answers.

Conclusions

Black *et al.* (2003) neatly sum up the characteristics of formative assessment as the use of assessment evidence to adapt teaching to meet learning needs:

> Formative assessment can occur many times in every lesson. It can involve several different methods for encouraging students to express what they are thinking and several different ways of acting on such evidence. It has to be within the control of the individual teacher and, for this reason, change in formative assessment practice is an integral part of a teacher's daily work. (p. 2)

The importance of discussing tasks with students, and of clarifying the success criteria for completing pieces of work, is central to the effectiveness of formative assessment (Dann 2002). Assessment procedures should be highlighted at the beginning of each task to give students the opportunity to talk to each other, as well as their teacher, about what will constitute appropriate performance. Such dialogue is particularly pertinent for those students who have previously 'failed' assessment tasks. It is obvious that teachers need to be clear about the purposes of the tasks they set and about what will constitute successful achievement.

Harlen (2008b, c) reiterates that the results of summative assessments can be used in various ways, whereas formative assessments have only one use: to help learning. Summative assessments serve a variety of purposes – to track student progress in schools, to inform parents, teachers and other stakeholders of student achievements, to certificate or accredit student learning, to select students for the next stage of their education. As we have already seen, the 'stakes' of such assessments vary – with summative testing through public examinations being of the highest stake because of the importance ascribed to the resultant data and the influence it has on teaching and the curriculum. Formative assessment enables the teacher to be more forward-looking and proactive, changing their approach to teaching based on what assessment evidence tells them of their students' needs. This is a process of gradually 'letting go' as students become empowered to direct their own learning, based on effective self-assessment and self-regulation.

6 | Marking, feedback and self-assessment – communicating the results of assessment

In this chapter, three related assessment activities – marking, providing feedback and self-assessing – are considered. The emphasis here is on communication, recognizing that assessment should not merely be a summative act, but a support to students' learning: a two-way process through which teachers develop a clear understanding of their students' educational needs, and students become aware of how to use assessment information to improve their attainment.

What do we hope to achieve by marking students' work? There are many different answers to this question, each reflecting specific assessment intentions – first, the teacher may simply wish to acknowledge that the student has completed a piece of work (often signified by a tick). This is the quickest, least sophisticated form of assessment, giving little helpful feedback to the student on his or her performance or guidance about where to go next. We might therefore conclude that effective marking should include at least some element of target setting. Second, marking can be a means of gauging each student's knowledge and understanding of a topic or theme at a particular time. Third, marking can strive to be motivational – supporting the students' efforts and pointing out the strengths, as well as the weaknesses, of their work. Constructive criticism is important, for without this, marking can quickly become de-motivational. Finally, on occasions, and as appropriate, marking may play a disciplinary role, particularly if a student has chosen not to engage with a task – such as failing to attempt their homework, or a piece of classwork (Butt 2005c). The reasons *why* this is the case need some consideration. Marking can therefore have a number of aims and functions – acknowledgement of work completed, monitoring knowledge and understanding, inspiring motivation, giving information, target setting and censuring. These are diverse, complex and conflicting demands; the expectations of the marking systems we use are therefore considerable.

Teachers spend a lot of time marking and we need to be confident that this time is being spent wisely. It may sound like heresy to criticize teachers who devote long hours to their marking, but if this activity lacks any real purpose it is effectively time wasted. Many teachers, particularly in the early years of their career, become overwhelmed by the sheer volume of marking expected of them. If marking only acknowledges that a student has 'had a go' at completing a piece of work, and the student subsequently gains little helpful intelligence about what or why they have done well (or badly), why bother? This is not a facetious question – why should any teacher spend large amounts of their time on an activity that apparently has little educational value? (Butt 2005c). Unfortunately, all too often teachers concentrate their marking efforts on what is easiest to assess, rather than on what has the greatest educative value for the child. For example, many teachers spend time correcting spelling, punctuation and grammar, rather than focusing directly on aspects of their students' knowledge and understanding of the curriculum subject. Too much time spent assessing presentation and neatness, rather than on the subject itself, is also misdirected. Better to have planned what should be assessed, considered why this assessment will be valid and what will constitute achievement at the lesson planning stage. Conveying this information to students obviously has considerable learning benefits.

Consider the reflective comments of Ruth Sutton as she looks back on her time spent marking as a new teacher:

> In my first year of teaching I had four examination classes . . . I also had several other classes of younger students, all of whose books had to be marked with reasonable frequency, but I got bogged down by it, and fell behind, so that work might be marked weeks after it was completed, when any feedback was no longer of interest to the children or of great relevance to their learning. Not infrequently, late in the evening, halfway through a pile of books or essays, which never seemed to diminish, I asked myself what was the point of it all. I knew that I had to recognise that the work had been read, but specific feedback demanded more than that. Without more careful scrutiny of what they'd done, I had little to say to them when work was

returned, they took less notice, and my dissatisfaction with the whole process grew. (Sutton, 1995, pp. 64–5, cited in Butt 2005c)

Clearly a more strategic use of time is essential here – a case of 'assessing less, better'. The intention must be to cut out any marking that is done for no real purpose. This is not advocating a casual 'way out' of teachers' marking commitments: what is required is a greater awareness of what assessment information is needed, how this will be shared with the students, and how to create appropriate assessment tasks. Less frequent, more targeted assessment which conveys useful educational information to the learner is the goal.

Marking as communication

One of the key considerations when assessing must be communication. The effectiveness of marking relies on students understanding what teachers 'mean' by the marks they award. This is an area of huge confusion and misconception, with teachers continuing with their marking regime for years without appreciating the communication gap that may exist between themselves and the learner. What do students understand by their teachers' grades or comments? Do they even read what has been written? Are they really expected to act upon advice? Do they need to show evidence of taking action? Can they set themselves, with support if necessary, educational targets using the teacher's marks and comments? (Butt 2005c).

Commenting on a research project initiated to investigate assessment for learning, Black *et al.* (2003) note that teachers added comments on their students' written work that did not really help them identify what they had achieved and what the next steps in their learning should be:

Most of the comments we saw . . . either stated a general evaluation, which indicated neither what had been achieved nor what steps to take next, or were geared to improving presentation or to merely completing work. Examples included; 'Good', 'Well done', 'Title?', 'Date?', 'Space out questions on the page', 'Rule off each piece of work', 'Use a pencil and a ruler for diagrams', 'Please finish' and 'Answer all the questions'. (p. 44)

In addition, grades and marks on their own do not inform students how to perform better, do not support the learning process, and either serve to inflate or deflate the individual's ego through competition with their peers. Better to indicate that all learners can do something to improve on previous performance, rather than to create groups of 'winners' and 'losers'. Figure 6.1, opposite, makes these points clear.

Weeden *et al.* (2002) provide a further helpful checklist of principles for marking and feedback:

♦ Marking should be linked to clear learning objectives.
♦ Assessments should be 'fit for purpose' and have appropriate mark schemes.
♦ Marking should help identify student misconceptions.
♦ Marking should be focused and prioritized.
♦ Marking needs to be planned for and integral to teaching and learning.
♦ Marking and feedback should take place quickly so that students remember the context.
♦ Recording may need to take a variety of forms that are manageable and informative. (p. 101)

It may be difficult for students to appreciate exactly what teachers are trying to convey in their brief written comments, or oral statements, about their work. After all, assessment feedback comes in a wide variety of forms – ticks, marks, grades, smiley faces, stickers, casual comments – all of which need to be correctly interpreted and understood by the learner. The confusion associated with understanding assessment feedback illustrates why it is often ineffectual in improving students' learning, and potentially damaging to motivation and self-esteem.

Monitoring, recording and reporting

Although teachers carry around much assessment information in their heads, they also need quick and reliable ways of 'capturing' important assessment data. This commonly involves using record books (markbooks) and/or computer files, which are likely to be the most substantial ongoing record of each student's performance. Many teachers aim to add to these records every time they formally

1. The criteria against which students' work is assessed should be clearly communicated and understood. Both the assessor and the assessed should be talking the same assessment language. The assessment criteria should link back to the learning objectives stated for the lesson.

2. The reason why marks have been awarded (or withheld) should be made clear to the student. What marks are awarded for should therefore be mutually understood. Often teachers award marks for both 'attainment' and 'effort' – this can create problems because gaining an objective appreciation of the effort each student has put into his or her work is difficult. Some students find work easy and complete it quickly and well; some may struggle for hours, only producing work of a poor standard. What does it mean to a student to be continually awarded high effort marks, but low attainment marks? Or vice versa?

3. When planning lessons, teachers need to consider what, and how, they will assess student learning. Will the focus for assessment be the students' grasp of new content? Or skills? Will credit be given for presentation? Will marks be taken away for poor punctuation, spelling and grammar? Is the intention to provide a written comment on each piece of work? To 'say' what? Is the student expected to respond to the comment? Will he or she understand what is being communicated?

4. The next educational steps should be apparent to the student. He or she should know, from the comments on a piece of assessed work, what has to be done to improve in terms of learning, attainment and assessment.

5. At the end of the assessment process the teacher should be confident about why he or she has awarded each mark to each student. It is a professional responsibility to be able to explain or justify why this mark has been given to this piece of work.

(Adapted from the Geographical Association website, www.geography. org,uk, cited in Butt 2005c)

Figure 6.1 Considerations when marking students' work

assess a student's work, or obtain significant and reliable evidence of a change in their performance. This information comes from either a permanent source, such as a piece of writing, or from an ephemeral source, such as the observation of a student working in a group.

Why do we collect assessment information?

What is a record of marks *for*? Recording marks and brief written comments can only advance children's learning if they are used intelligently. Teachers must therefore have clear intentions about what they will record, and why. There are three broad purposes to keeping such records:

◆ *To monitor progress*. For example, to show the extent to which work has been completed by students – its content coverage, the context of skills work, etc. – and to provide the basis for a detailed summative report to be compiled for the parent/carer, next teacher, school management or OfSTED. This assessment information can also be used to inform future plans for teaching and reflect on the success of teaching.
◆ *To inform other people*. For example, to provide subject-specific analyses of next steps for individual students and for other teachers – feeding forward to the next topic or learning activities
◆ *To show that certain important things are happening*. For example, to demonstrate that work has been prepared and marked, thus fulfilling accountability purposes. (Butt 2006c)

The ways in which assessment records might be used have implications for the types of assessment tasks set. Schools often have clear guidelines for staff about the nature and form of the records they wish to be kept, which may be laid down in school and department policies. These partly dictate the types of marks awarded and the record completed for particular pieces of work, for this information will need to have a common currency and be easily organized such that whole school analysis can be carried out (Butt 2006c). Informal systems of recording assessment information can also be kept by teachers, but it is time-consuming to run two parallel recording systems – one official and one unofficial. Grades or numerical marks cannot possibly cover all these purposes: therefore many teachers add qualitative written notes which address wider issues, such as the impact of an upsetting home event or the emergence of an increasingly co-operative attitude. No single example of 'what works' in terms of a record book's layout exists, since this will vary according to the age and ability of the students, the subject/s taught, and the requirements of the department and/or school. However, the basic expectations of a recording system are that it captures the students' assessment grades/marks, the types of assessment used, the context, focus and date of the assessments, and provides comments on how this information will affect future planning. Some teachers' records also show 'ticks' for attendance and work satisfactorily completed, percentages for exam or test results, notes on particular students' special needs, and effort grades (Butt 2006c).

Whatever record system is used, it should provide reliable information about each student's knowledge, understanding and skills in a form that can be easily translated (and understood) by the student, other teachers and parents/carers. This flexibility is necessary if suitable assessment information is to be provided for different contexts – such as parents' evenings, departmental meetings, profiles of achievement, or target setting. It should also be possible, by simple aggregation of marks, to create an overall assessment of each student's level/s of attainment.

The perception that recording marks is largely a fruitless activity can result in a reluctance to go one step further and use assessment data to make a difference to students' learning. However, where schools have systematized their collection and use of data from teachers – often in combination with commercially produced performance measures such as MIDYIS (Middle Years Information System), YELLIS (Year 11 Information System) and CATs (Cognitive Abilities Test) – the impact on student learning is often impressive. Monitoring students' performance in this way helps to identify those who are under-achieving, those who are 'coasting', and those who have shown a sudden change in their assessed performance (either up or down).

Portfolios

Portfolios, or collections of samples of students' assessed work, provide exemplification of student attainment standards. There is no formal requirement to collect students' work in this way, but portfolios can be used for making judgements about levels of performance and to provide evidence of progression. In combination with materials which exemplify performance standards, such as those on the QCDA website (www.qcda.gov.uk), portfolios can provide a check that assessment standards are in line with national standards.

A variety of different types of portfolios is used in schools:

◆ *Department portfolio* – used in secondary schools and designed to provide exemplars of students' work completed on a range of activities against which consistent judgements of performance can be made. Such portfolios therefore exemplify the department's judgements about the standards which need to be achieved for the award of a particular National Curriculum level.

◆ *Class portfolios* – these provide a record of the activities and achievements of a particular class and aid the curriculum review process. Common assessment activities, used across all the subject classes within a year group, might be collected into a class portfolio to enable comparisons across teaching groups.

◆ *Individual student portfolios* – frequently updated portfolios, where a small set of exemplars of a particular student's achievements are kept. Such portfolios should see a 'turnover' of work and be used to support summative assessments of performance, or as a discussion document to be used with the student, other teachers and/or parents to help the formative development of that student. (Butt 2006c)

Portfolios can often be used with a range of audiences and for a variety of purposes. For example, portfolios can:

◆ serve as a reference point for all teachers in promoting and supporting consistent judgements both during, and at the end of, a Key Stage;

◆ be used as a focus for moderation between schools;

◆ support new colleagues in informing their understanding and judgement of students' work;

◆ remove the pressure on individual teachers to compile their own collection of work to support their judgements;

◆ demonstrate to others (e.g. parents, other teachers, students, governors, OfSTED) the agreed standards of work within the school;

- exemplify progression, support evaluation and help review the school's curriculum; and
- include work from a small number of 'case study' students, showing a range of work and attainment at different assessment levels.

Materials collected in portfolios should have a small comment sheet attached for the teacher who has selected the work to record the context or focus of the sample. In addition, annotations recording significant features of the performance of each student on this task, a brief summary to show the extent to which this work has fulfilled expectations, and an indication of how or why the teacher's judgement has been made, are all useful. To save time it is advisable to collect only a few pieces of exemplar materials, but to annotate these carefully. Students can be asked to complete self-evaluation slips that can be included in personal portfolios (Butt 2006c).

Reporting assessment information

Although the legal requirements on schools to keep records of students' progress are minimal, there are statutory requirements to report progress annually to parents/carers. These reports are often supplemented with some form of half-year, or even term, reports and with other strategies such as using homework diaries (completed by students, signed weekly by parents, and monitored by teachers). These constitute a more frequent means of monitoring, recording and reporting assessment information.

Annual written reports usually contain the following information:

- A comment on the student's progress (in each subject and activity) highlighting their strengths and needs.
- An overall comment on general progress.
- A record of attendance.
- A statement about how the parent/carer can respond to the report, if they wish.

The requirements to provide National Curriculum Levels for a student at the end of Key Stages 1, 2 and 3, as well as assessment levels awarded through SATs (where these still exist) and levels ascribed through teacher assessments (where these apply) are statutory, as is the target grade for GCSE at the end of Year 10. Schools also have to report against the Early Learning Goals at the end of the Foundation Stage. Each school has to report to parents/carers (i) whether any assessments have been disapplied; (ii) comparative whole-school data for other students' performance in different curricular areas (as a percentage); (iii) a comment about what the results show for each student's progress and performance; and (iv) a statement on national performance levels in English, Maths and Science. Schools often add further information to their reports. Many parents find this plethora of information daunting, even though it is supplied with good intentions. Schools therefore have a responsibility to help parents make sense of it all (Butt 2006c).

Writing comments in reports that could apply to any number of students (e.g. 'making sound progress', 'satisfactory work this year'), or which give little guidance about how to improve performance and attainment, is pointless. Almost all parents are very interested in their children's progress and wish to know about their strengths and weaknesses, how they could improve, whether they are behaving appropriately, and how they are involved in school life. To this end the best reports are rigorous, user-friendly and precise about student performance, while also giving clear guidance for the future.

Giving assessment feedback

With its potential to support the learning process and promote student achievement, assessment feedback has been acknowledged as a positive and powerful educational tool. The term 'feedback' originates from simple flow diagrams employed to describe production processes, such as within manufacturing industry or agriculture. Here the simplest form of system might be described as follows:

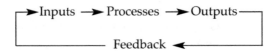

Feedback is used to keep systems 'on track' and as a means of regulating performance and production – although this is rarely as simple, complete or closed, as this model implies. The principle within educational assessment is that feedback enables current and previous (assessment) information to be used to help shape future learning, performance and outcomes. This has a clear link to achieving targets (see Chapter 7) where we have a desired educational outcome for students and we use assessment information to make sure this is achieved.

Traditionally, feeding back assessment information has been a one-way process, from teacher to student. However, many forms and directions of feedback exist – from student to teacher, from student to student (often related to peer assessment) and from student to him- or herself (self-assessment). If we broaden the perspective to encapsulate a much wider conception of feedback, we can see that many other stakeholders could also be involved in the process. As we have seen, these include the passing of assessment information to other teachers, parents/carers, other educational institutions, employers and inspectors. The correct timing of feedback is essential. If it is to support the next steps of learning it needs to be done relatively quickly – or else the student will have largely forgotten what was being assessed, or will have already moved on, stood still or regressed. The danger is that if feedback is delayed, incorrect assumptions, understandings or skills can become embedded. But, ironically, if feedback is too immediate it can promote dependency.

As Swaffield (2008) concludes:

> If feedback is geared towards improving learning rather than measuring it, if it puts the emphasis on each student's progress and avoids comparison amongst students, if it is part of ongoing dialogue rather than a judgement delivered by the teacher after the event and if there is the expectation that feedback is acted upon, it is likely that feedback will make a positive contribution to learning rather than a negative one. (p. 69)

Written comments on completed work probably constitute the most common form of assessment feedback the majority of students receive, as well as the most variable in terms of quality and impact. Marking may simply record that a piece of work has been completed (a 'tick'), may be entirely summative (a numerical score or grade), or may include a written judgement or advice (a brief comment). Research suggests that students rarely 'take in' the written comments teachers add to their work – particularly if these comments tend to say the same things on each piece of work assessed – preferring to simply compare grades with their peers. Comments also tend to be short and summative, rather than giving feedback on *how* to improve. If the teacher does not bring the students' attention to these comments – explaining them, expecting action to be taken in response to them, and reinforcing their formative importance – he or she cannot expect students to take them seriously. Much of the time that teachers spend writing comments on students' work is wasted if they have little direct impact on students' *learning*.

Because written feedback often has little formative impact, we need to find ways of making it more effective – here the adage of 'assess less, better' is again important. Writing comments is necessary to help assess work that is new, different, unusual or challenging, rather than for work that involves simple factual recall. These comments might celebrate what has been done well and, more importantly, point the way to improved performance in the future. This approach is far more successful in advancing learning than providing a whole term's worth of short, repetitive and largely ineffectual platitudes about each student's performance. Importantly, longer, more detailed, more analytical comments, produced every three or four weeks, will actually take less time for the teacher to produce. However, they will have a greater effect on student learning, especially if the teacher can find time to reinforce them orally. Planning is obviously key, for the teacher needs to space out appropriate activities and key assessment opportunities to ensure that not all teaching groups reach a major 'assessment point' at the same time. This also gives students a chance to show that they have understood and responded to the teacher's feedback before the next key assessment task.

Formative assessment must give students something to 'do' and think about, rather than simply offering judgements. Look at the following comments:

A. Complete the table and remember to label the diagram.
B. Once you've completed the table, think about why the figures in the third column are increasing so rapidly. What does this tell you about the rate of natural increase? What factors would reduce these figures? Also, you've missed out two labels on the diagram – complete these and write two sentences to explain

their importance to the process of population growth. Think about the connections between birth rate, death rate, natural increase and migration in determining population size.

Essentially the comments in 'A' merely require a task to be finished off; those in 'B' also expect this, but in addition they prompt the student to think. Sometimes it may be possible to set individual targets in these comments, such as 'Next time you write about such data, include some of the figures in your writing to illustrate your points and give more detail' (Butt 2006b).

Black *et al.* (2003), reflecting on research undertaken by Ruth Butler (Butler 1988) into the effectiveness of teachers' marks, consider the impact of using combinations of both marks and comments, noting that the learning gains are greatest when only comments are used. This finding was surprising, particularly as most teachers adopt a 'marks and comments' approach. Teachers who shifted to using only comments justified their practice as follows:

◆ Students rarely read comments, preferring to compare marks with peers as their first reaction on getting work back.
◆ Teachers rarely give students time in class to read comments that are written on work, and probably few, if any, students return to consider these at home.
◆ Often the comments are brief and/or not specific, for example 'Details?'.
◆ The same written comments frequently recur in a student's book, implying that students do not take note of or act on the comments. (Black *et al.* 2003, p. 43)

The practicalities of assessment feedback

We have seen that giving effective feedback to students about their performance is not necessarily straightforward. First, there is an issue about the number of students each teacher has to feed back to – it is not uncommon for there to be more than 25 students in a class, making it extremely difficult for the teacher to provide individualized comments to everyone during oral feedback. Most teachers therefore provide 'generic' oral feedback to all the class after assessing their work, but save specific comments for individuals (who may have performed or attained particularly well or badly), giving such guidance on relatively few occasions. Some teachers try to provide individualized oral comments to, say, five students each lesson creating a 'rotation' of personal feedback. This requires good organization and may not actually coincide with the time when a specific student needs most help, or when particular assessment issues arise. However, it does get over the problem of some students *never* receiving feedback from the teacher, this being directed to more 'needy' (or perhaps more visible) cases. Second, feeding back to students needs to be handled sensitively – particularly if this is done orally, in front of their peers. Many students take such feedback very personally, interpreting the teacher's comments as a criticism of themselves as individuals, rather than as a positive attempt to improve their performance as learners. Interestingly this applies as much to praising student performance as criticizing it, for many students will be embarrassed if their work is singled out as being better than their peers, or used as an example of what others in the class should aspire to achieve. Just as in good classroom management, where one might choose to target the behaviour that requires attention rather than the qualities of the person who initiates that behaviour, then our focus in assessment feedback should be on the assessment task. Third, teachers need to understand the ways in which individual students are motivated to perform better. Assessment feedback must be differentiated according to how students are motivated. Some may need a 'push' to achieve more, which could be stimulated by setting up competition among their peers; some may need to be told that their performance is improving (or otherwise) against their own personal 'best'; others may need a 'quiet word' or, alternatively, public praise to continue to achieve (Butt 2006b). Few people perform better by being continually told they are *not* achieving. Dweck (1999) focuses on motivational and esteem issues, identifying two types of feedback: (i) that which identifies the student as a 'good' or 'bad' achiever (usually on the basis of marks, ranking, grades, etc.) – often with negative effects on student motivation and esteem; and (ii) that which focuses on the strengths or weaknesses of a particular piece of work, rather than on the students themselves – often with positive effects generated through encouraging the students, no matter what their previous achievements have been, to see where they can perform better. The first type of feedback tends to be negative because it discourages low attainers, it also tends to make high attainers avoid taking risks or grasping new opportunities to learn. Here the fear of failure makes 'risk taking' unwise, particularly if students are unsure about their potential success. Lastly, feedback should indicate how to bridge the gap between current performance and successful achievement in the future.

Student self-assessment

If students are to produce work that responds successfully to clearly stated learning aims and outcomes, they need a sound understanding of both the assessment system and of teacher expectations. To become more autonomous, students must achieve a greater self-awareness of their work. That is, instead of the *teacher* constantly telling the students what is 'good' or 'bad' about the work they produce – and how to improve it – the *students* themselves must increasingly take this responsibility. Self-assessment will make the teacher's role easier as students 'correct' themselves before they hand in their work. This is perhaps the ultimate goal of formative assessment, but it requires the student to 'do more'. Sadler (1989) captures this point well when he states that for students to improve they must be able to 'monitor the quality of their own work during production' (p. 199). This, of course, relies on the students being able to appreciate what standards are required of a finished piece of work. They also need to be objective in measuring the quality of what they produce against the standards for acceptability the teacher sets. This is also self-assessment. Here students have a clear concept of the expectations placed upon them, of the standards underpinning high quality work, and of how these are expressed through the process of assessment. This is an important aspect of *ipsative* assessment, where the progress each child makes is measured against their own previous levels of performance and attainment, rather than against the group they are learning with. Sutton (1995) argues that students need to believe that they are capable of learning, before they will be able to gainfully self-assess. This may seem like an odd point to make: surely everybody believes they are capable of learning? However, when one talks to disillusioned students who feel that school is 'not for them', one of the main reasons they cite is the belief that they are largely incapable of learning what is taught. If these students are asked to self-assess they will often state that they see no point in learning what the school offers them, are bored by the process of learning, or simply find lessons too difficult. Self-assessment also relies on students being able to set realistic and achievable learning targets for themselves, which they are capable of achieving within their 'extended grasp'. Challenge is important, but this challenge has to be structured in such a way as to ensure that the student is confident that their effort and commitment will be rewarded. Most importantly, students must not be afraid to fail. Failure is acceptable, as long as the learner can assess the reasons why he or she has failed and understands how to perform better in the future.

Establishing a regime for the introduction and application of student self-assessment is initially very teacher-centred. It is the teacher who knows the subject curriculum, specification and/or syllabus, who is the expert in both the subject and educational practice, and who appreciates the role that assessment must play in the educational development of the child. Elements of this knowledge, understanding and skill must be clearly conveyed to students to enable them to have a sensible input into the assessment process. In a sense, enabling students to take responsibility for their own assessment is a process of letting go, where teachers relinquish many of their traditional assessment roles as the sole arbiters of student performance to establish a more student-centred emphasis on self- and peer assessment. This is not to say that teachers will no longer assess work, but that students will have to adopt greater responsibility and independence in helping to shape their educational futures.

Self- and peer assessment is not easy. Being honest about how one is performing, and more importantly having a reasonable sense of what one has to do to get better, is challenging. Often 'more able' students understand what is required quite readily – in fact they have probably adopted successful self-assessment procedures from a comparatively early stage in their learning, and have been rewarded by achieving good marks. They clearly understand what they have achieved and how they have achieved it, applying principles of self-assessment to their own work before handing it in for marking. They may also enquire why their work is not up to standard if they perform poorly. 'Less able' students often do not have this ability, confidence or motivation. Supporting children such that they make realistic and accurate judgements of their accomplishments, neither being too harsh or too lenient in their views, obviously takes sensitivity and time. Assessment practices in other subjects also have an influence. Starting children within a self-assessment regime from an early age has benefits – schools which adopt these principles across the board obviously have advantages. Self-assessment should therefore help children take more control of the learning process and make them feel embedded in what they do, rather than education being experienced as something that is simply done to them. However, the influence of common practice is difficult to change – many children, when introduced to self-assessment methods, question the appropriateness of their involvement ('It's the teacher's job to assess us'), or fail to see how this will help them learn ('I don't know how to do it, that's why I ask the teacher'). There are also time implications – at the start, these techniques are time-consuming and difficult to establish, but once they become commonly accepted and understood they have a liberating effect. They free teachers from the excessive time spent marking all the children's work and from being the sole assessor, while shifting some of the responsibility of the assessment process on to the students themselves. As a result students become more engaged and autonomous learners who do not simply raise their hands for the teacher to sort out their problems, but look for their own solutions.

Some principles and techniques for self- and peer assessment

Weeden *et al.* (2002) state some strategies that can be applied to promote self-assessment:

◆ *Clarify the assessment criteria for students* – Students can be very effective at self- (and peer) assessment, but must be able to identify what they are trying to assess and what constitutes having met the teacher's assessment criteria. Communicating in 'student speak' what the assessment criteria mean and what appropriate work looks like is very important. We should not underestimate the challenge that this presents – for assessment criteria in the National Curriculum and for external examinations can be complex.

◆ *Clarify the learning objectives for students* – Students should have a (broad) sense of the purpose of each lesson, the content to be covered and how their learning will be assessed. They will only be able to effectively self-assess if each of these is known to them.

◆ *Establish some key self-assessment questions* – Such as: What do I think I have learned? What do I still need to learn? What did I find easy/hard and why? What should I do in the future to improve my learning? Initially responses to such questions will be short and simple, but with guidance, students can be encouraged to think more deeply about what these questions are really asking about their learning and how to move themselves forward.

◆ *Support the act of self-assessment* – Students can be provided with structured review sheets which reflect learning outcomes and detail particular aspects of their work that require assessment. Students can be asked to judge how well they think they have done, how hard they found particular activities, and what they think they need to do to move forward in their learning.

◆ *Model examples of assessed work* – Anonymized examples of previous students' work can be provided for similar tasks, having gained permission from the students, to show what constitutes good, average and poor work. By talking through, or annotating, this work the teacher can enable students to begin to understand what principles are applied to the assessment process. Students can then begin to apply these to their own work. This helps students to see assessment through the teacher's eyes and to emulate the actions of an expert assessor.

◆ *Facilitate discussion about assessment* – Assessment decisions can be facilitated between the teacher and the whole group of students; the teacher and individual students; and between the students themselves. Genuine discussion – involving all those in the classroom, rather than being teacher-dominated – is important to the learning process, particularly where it involves students thinking about their thinking (metacognition).

Capturing the outcomes of self-assessment can be problematic. Some teachers provide their students with self-assessment proformas, but these can be tedious and time-consuming to complete. There is a danger that filling in such forms can become routinized, with students filling in similar, easily achievable targets from one lesson to the next. There is also evidence that some students are confused as to what they should write and how they should act upon advice (Weeden *et al.* 2002). This suggests that records of achievement portfolios – kept by the teacher or the student, but with an input from both – may be more helpful. These can be combined with 'interviews' with students, or even the completion of small journals by the learner.

The use of peer assessment, which applies the same principles as self-assessment, can also improve educational performance and attainment. Peer assessment is another valuable student-centred approach in the drive towards achieving effective assessment for learning. Giving students responsibility to assess the work of others may initially appear daunting; there may be fears that students will be overly critical of their peers (or overly generous) and that they will not take the process seriously. But evidence suggests that this is not usually the case and that students soon realize that they must be fair and constructive with each other if they expect to be treated in the same ways themselves. The process also helps them achieve a clearer understanding of what they don't yet know in terms of assessment and to start to bridge the gaps that still exist. Peer assessment therefore tends to have a positive impact on the students' efforts of self-assessment.

Conclusions

Marking students' work is not the end of the assessment process, it is the start. Organizing and using assessment information with a variety of audiences is crucial and highlights the importance of monitoring, recording and reporting. Feedback can be on the task completed – designed to help students correct any misconceptions about knowledge and understanding; on the process – how to do the task, whether it is appropriate to seek help; and on the performance of the individual – related to motivation, effort and interest. If all three are addressed, the feedback will arguably be most successful, teaching students how to manage their work, solve problems and realistically appraise their performance. If feedback is personal but negative ('You must work harder', 'You just don't try', 'Poor effort') then the likelihood is that the learner has their ego dented, does not receive any idea about how to improve their performance and seeks ways to mask or qualify their underperformance. Casual personal praise will be similarly flawed, as it does nothing to help the student understand why they have done well on this task, or how to make future improvements.

Effective feedback is highly situational, it depends on the context in which it is given. More importantly it depends on the students themselves – are they ready to receive, understand and trust what is being said? Are they empowered and motivated to act on this information? Increasing learner autonomy is the key, for students need to make sense of the formative assessment message, not simply expect the teacher to always tell them what to do.

7 | Achieving assessment targets

What is a target? A general definition of a target is a point to aim at: it is therefore often understood as an objective which we should like to achieve. This implies that we must first identify a 'goal' and then aim to reach it (or, perhaps more literally, to 'hit' it) through taking some form of action. This chapter explores what targets are used for in education, the setting of realistic targets and the assessment of students' progress towards achieving them (Butt 2006d).

When a target is set for a particular student, or group of students, we are communicating a particular desired level of performance, achievement or attainment we want them to reach – usually within a given timeframe (a few lessons, a few weeks, a term, or a year). This target may be of our own choosing, may be determined by a curriculum or syllabus, may be established by our school, or may be negotiated individually with the student. It is usually expressed in words, but is often supported by data. Targets are identified using a range of sources of evidence of the students' current strengths and weaknesses, but often culminate in statements of expected assessed outcomes. There are also national targets for student attainment established by the government in the UK (Butt 2006d).

Setting a target implies a commitment, by both teacher and student, to make the necessary effort to achieve changes in current levels of performance. Target-setting therefore links closely to assessment – student achievement needs to be accurately measured at the start of the process and then re-assessed, once interventions have been made, against the particular target set. The idea is that by first measuring and then focusing student performance on realistic targets, improvements can be achieved (Butt 2006d). The Attainment Targets and Level Descriptions used in the National Curriculum provide strong indicators of the importance of target-setting (and getting) in schools.

The purposes of target-setting are therefore easily stated:

85

◆ To use sources of information, including attainment data, to focus plans on raising standards of pupil attainment.
◆ To ensure that pupils' prior attainment and achievement is built upon throughout the Key Stage.
◆ To identify and focus teaching on areas of underperformance.
◆ To actively support improved learning outcomes for under-achieving groups of pupils. (DfES 2004b)

In order to successfully establish and track target 'setting and getting' some teachers and schools apply the acronym SMART to their targeting: that is, targets should be Specific, Measurable, Achievable, Relevant and Time-related.

However, many educationists are deeply sceptical about the value of using assessment data in this context, either to set targets or to predict future student performance. Mary Jane Drummond (2008) asserts:

> Particularly dangerous, in my view, is the apparent built-in assumption that defining, labelling or measuring what a child can do today (or, more often, cannot do) is a completely reliable predictor of what she or he will do tomorrow – or at the moment of the next statutory assessment. If, however benevolent our intentions, we fall into a habit of thinking that the present dictates the future, that current achievement is commensurate with so-called ability, a fixed and unreachable entity within each child, that children's so-called levels of achievement at the age of four or five, or six or seven, tell us anything about what is to happen in the future, we are colluding in a deterministic and profoundly anti-educational enterprise. Our priorities should be to fight the predictions that the bean-counters make on our behalf, not to concur with them. (p. 11)

Initially, target-setting is extremely dependent on the teacher, less so on the student. But if targets are not negotiated with the student then they are not 'owned' by them, existing as something imposed from above which the student may not feel appropriate or important. At its worst, the process of target-setting can be mechanistic and sterile, largely unrelated to learning but more closely tied to bureaucratic assessment demands. For these reasons many students, particularly lower attainers, do not see the point of target-setting.

Target-setting in schools

Statutory target-setting in the National Curriculum began in schools in England and Wales in 1998 (Key Stages 2 and 4) and 2001 (Key Stage 3). In secondary schools governing bodies were made responsible for reporting targets to their Local Authority (LA) each December for Year 8 and Year 10 students, which then allowed the school five terms to meet the targets before students were externally assessed (through SATs or GCSEs). Additionally, most schools also set 'internal' targets for student performance in each subject (Butt 2006d).

Data on student performance is produced annually by the DCSF, OfSTED and QCDA and fed into schools in the Autumn term. This data allows each school to compare its performance across Key Stages with similar schools. Data is generated on student performance at a range of scales and can be used for either educational or bureaucratic purposes. Assessment data therefore plays a central role in the process of setting targets, but can initially appear daunting to teachers who may fear that it will be used out of context. Target-setting is currently very important to governments, who make public commitments about educational standards and the levels of performance of young people in their nation's schools. Such targets are significant because they can be used to hold teachers, students and the government itself to account for the progress being made within the education system. In this respect, targets that are set for educational attainment nationally must be realistic, reasonable, achievable and set within an appropriate timeframe.

National targets in England and Wales

As an illustrative example of national target-setting in England and Wales, the government previously established for itself the following targets for 14-year-olds to achieve:

◆ By 2007: 85 per cent of 14-year-olds achieve Level 5 or above in English and Mathematics tests (80 per cent in Science tests) nationally, with this level of performance sustained until 2008.
◆ In 2007, 74 per cent of pupils nationally reached Level 5 or above in KS3 English, 76 per cent reached Level 5 in Mathematics, 73 per cent reached Level 5 in Science.

◆ By 2007: 85 per cent of 14-year-olds achieve Level 5 or above in Information and Communication Technology (ICT) Teacher Assessments nationally, with this level of performance sustained until 2008.

◆ In 2007, 74 per cent of pupils nationally reached Level 5 or above in KS3 ICT TA, compared to 71 per cent in 2006. (DCSF 2007, p. 2)

Such targets are laid down by law and each school is required to make provision for their achievement – that is, schools are required to clearly outline to students the expectations for their performance. Similar targets are also set for subjects at all stages of the students' education, as well as for their performance in external examinations – where the measure of standards regularly applied to secondary schools is the percentage of students who achieve five 'good' (that is, above grade C) GCSEs. This percentage tends to be applied as a yardstick to measure each secondary school's performance against other schools, locally and nationally. It is also a basis for any target set for whole-school improvement. Similar targets and measures of performance were previously applied with respect to students' achievement of particular SATs levels in primary and secondary schools (Butt 2006d). The recent scrapping of almost all SATs testing has largely removed this assessment data as a source of such target-setting. There is an obvious necessity to set national targets responsibly, with a realistic appreciation of what can be achieved. The creation of targets that are 'political', being overly aspirational and almost certainly unachievable within a given timeframe, creates an inflated and illusory expectation of performance. Empirical evidence, using previous results and realistic projections of improvement, must be employed. Neither schools nor students benefit from targets being set that reflect political whim, panic or the hasty introduction of rafts of new initiatives in an attempt to stimulate an immediate spike in assessment results.

At the whole-school level, target-setting regularly involves the analysis of massive amounts of assessment data. Most of this data is unique to the school and can enable a detailed appreciation of student performance. Each school can consider data from other schools within the Local Authority, as well as comparable data available nationally. The setting of targets obviously has an impact on individual students, and can be 'fine grained' by using single student performance data. Commercially available software can allow schools to import and analyse their own students' performance data against national data, to analyse students' answers to particular questions, to assess value added and to set targets (Butt 2006d). Performance can therefore be considered down to the level of small groups of students (say, low-achieving boys), individual students – and individual teachers.

Target-setting for students

Considerable emphasis is given to targeting the performance of underachieving students, as well as students for whom a small improvement in their performance will have beneficial effects for both them and their school (such as raising the performance of students currently on the grade C to D borderline at GCSE). Despite the government's commitment to meeting the needs of every child, there are often tangible differences in how target-setting and support is delivered according to different students' abilities. This is perhaps understandable – with limited time and resources available it is necessary to take a strategic approach to setting and achieving targets (Butt 2006d).

The DfES previously suggested the following whole-school approach to tackling underperformance at Key Stage 3 through the use of targets:

1. *Review:* Identify strengths, weaknesses and lessons learned from students' previously assessed performance. Review progress of current KS3 students – identify those on target to meet or exceed national expectations at the end of Year 9; identify groups or individual students who are not making sufficient progress, or who are at risk of 'failing'.
2. *Plan:* Adapt schemes of work and teaching plans to address weaknesses shared by many students. Create an intervention plan, set targets and organize support for students at risk.
3. *Implement:* Implement revised schemes of work and teaching plans. Ensure subject teams, year teams and support staff work collaboratively to implement the plan.
4. *Monitor and evaluate:* Monitor the implementation. Track students' progress towards their targets, particularly those receiving additional support. Evaluate the impact of the revised

schemes of work, teaching plans and intervention plan and adjust as necessary. (Adapted from DfES 2004b, cited in Butt 2006d)

At the classroom level, national and local data of student performance can be used to help set targets. However, there is also a mass of assessment data that is already 'in front of you' that can be used for setting your targets – assessed work from your students, ephemeral teacher assessments, test and exam results, observations, moderation of work across the department or school, and subject reports. All of these sources of evidence can combine to build up a picture of what are appropriate, achievable, realistic and timely targets to set.

Target-setting is a professional activity, usually performed at departmental and individual class level. It must value the professional judgement of teachers and should be based on accurate summative and formative assessment practices. In many schools the setting of targets is part of a system of monitoring and evaluating student performance, sometimes referred to as an 'improvement cycle' (see Figure 7.1).

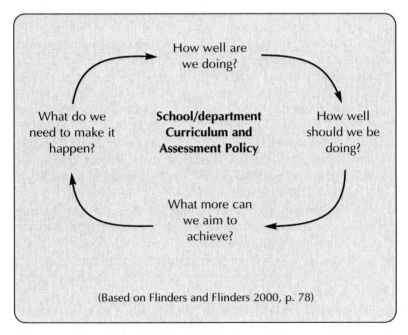

(Based on Flinders and Flinders 2000, p. 78)

Figure 7.1 An Improvement Cycle

Flinders and Flinders (2000) draw an important distinction between *forecasts* and targets. Forecasts are what a school, department, teacher or student might reasonably be expected to achieve based on measures of current practice and performance. Targets are essentially forecasts, but with the important addition of a degree of *challenge* – which may be modest or ambitious according to circumstances – designed to drive up standards. Target-setting uses a range of diagnostic and predictive data systems (such as MIDYIS (Years 7, 8 and 9), YELLIS (Year 11), NFER data (CATS test scores), Fischer Family Trust, Pupil Level Annual School Census (PLASC) etc.) alongside comparative data, from the school (Butt 2006d). These are combined with assessment information gathered in the classroom (or department) which takes into account the strengths, weaknesses and potential of individual students. All of this data should be considered within the context of the school's general performance levels and any information available on its overall achievements and expectations, such as OfSTED reports. It is important that whatever targets are set, based on this wealth of information, are realistic and achievable. There is no point in setting targets that are clearly unattainable given the context of the levels of resource input and the nature of the school (Butt 2006d).

Target-setting should be related to plans which aim to improve student learning. Such a process often refers to the setting of 'curricular targets' – targets in which numerical and descriptive data are translated into an achievable outcome, often involving specific teaching and learning objectives. The DfES represented this process as follows:

Information gathering (evidence base from which areas for improvement are identified) > **information analysis** (identification of areas of weakness which provide the basis for establishing curricular targets) > **action planning** (intervention, support and monitoring – activities that work towards achieving curricular targets) > **success criteria** (the possible outcomes for specific cohorts of students that will show that targets have been achieved). (Adapted from DfES 2004a, cited in Butt 2006d)

Targets, particularly short-term targets, should be shared with students in an appropriate form. Many departments will set up a spreadsheet as a means of tracking performance against the targets set – processing the data into graphs, tables, averages, aggregates or statistical diagrams, as appropriate. Spreadsheets might show current level of performance, test scores, external data as well as target grades/levels and records of teacher-assessed work.

Within early childhood education Carr (2001) introduces us to a technique of 'targeting' achievement through the use of narrative. Drawing on the work of early years' educators in New Zealand she shows how teachers built up 'learning stories' for each of their students on a day-to-day basis, based on a narrative of their achievements. The principle which underpins such stories is that they recognize the individuality of the learner and seek to give credit for what they can do. The story is comprehensive, including accounts of learning at home, engaging whole families in the learning and assessment process. Here the view of learning is holistic, recognizing that it cannot be easily broken down into lists of areas, content, skills and abilities to be learnt. As Drummond (2008) notes with reference to the teachers in New Zealand who use this approach:

> Their construction of learning is very different; they see it as a moving event, dynamic and changeful, practically synonymous with living. They see no need to restrict their assessment to the building blocks of literacy or numeracy: the learning stories are comprehensive in their scope. (p. 14)

Clarke (1998), cited in Drummond (2008), makes the important point that targets are most meaningful and relevant to students if they are set from *their* starting points, rather than being filtered down from the objectives and goals of teachers and senior managers in schools. Here students have to be able to see short-term, achievable steps within the targets, which must be carefully constructed to match their particular needs as reflected by their current performance levels.

Target-getting

Once achievable and realistic targets have been set, teachers and students have to go about meeting them. It is important that 'target-getting' is not just a paper exercise of juggling data – interventions in the educational process are necessary to achieve the targets set. There is a very real danger that the process of target-getting does not proceed to its final stages – therefore short-, medium- and long-term targets need to be identified and monitored. Data can be gathered and analysed, target grades or levels set, and proposed interventions discussed and recorded. However, if teachers and students do not *act* on these, then the targets will not be achieved. This highlights the importance of recognizing non-numerical targets and clearly outlining what action needs to be taken, by whom, and at what points. Periodic monitoring and assessment are key to this strategic process, through which the need for particular interventions (such as continuing professional development of teachers) to improve teaching and learning are uncovered (Butt 2006d).

It is clear that monitoring the progress of students towards their achievement of targets is particularly important. According to the nature of their target(s) this may take different forms: summarizing the assessment information gathered since establishing the target and making a judgement as to whether the target set will be met in the timescale outlined is essential. This indicates whether students are on track. It will usually involve bringing together relevant teacher assessment information (from records of awarded marks and comments), information from end-of-unit or course assessments, test results and ephemeral evidence. Butt (2006d) asserts that judgements can then be made as to whether key learning objectives are being met (or 'worked towards') and the most accurate 'best fit' of performance against levels, criteria or grades.

As Harlen (2008a) states:

> Openness about goals and criteria for assessment not only helps students to direct their effort appropriately but removes the secrecy from the process of summative assessment, enabling them to recognize their own role in their achievement instead of it being the result of someone else's decisions. (p. 145)

Conclusions

The setting of targets has always gone on in schools. Traditionally, teachers have carried with them a professional appreciation of where individuals and groups of students should 'be' within their learning – particularly as they have progressed towards 'high stakes' assessment points. They have also had good ideas about how to address problems in their students' progress to ensure that targets are met. What is currently different is the scale and level of investment in target-setting and target-getting in schools. The recording of the achievement of set targets, as well as the assessed performance of students, is a more open publicly accountable exercise than in the past. Meeting targets is an annual, national expectation for the education sector – with ever more elaborate means of ensuring that neither students nor teachers fall by the wayside. However, we must not lose sight of Black and Wiliam's (1998a) assertion that grades and levels do not, of themselves, motivate students to improve their performance – feedback from teachers needs to be personal, inclusive and practical to ensure such changes (Butt 2006d).

The nature of the assessments that focus on target-setting and target-getting are not closely connected to the learning process. They are not interested in what students learn on a day-to-day basis, being more concerned on predicting future performance and on highlighting particular areas of student cognitive strength or weakness that might be developed. As such, many of the cognitive ability tests (and data) currently used in schools claim to be able to identify under-performing students and predict future performance in GCSEs and AS/A levels. Whether this information is valid, and what is done with the information, is something which each school and teacher must decide.

Using assessment data for target-setting can be an expansive process. School managers are keen on analysing data to see how their school, departments, staff and students compare with others. This may involve a self-evaluation by the school to indicate areas for further development, or a more fine-grained approach to performance management at the departmental, staff or student level. Context is always important in target-setting – one has to compare 'like with like', and as such the assessment data that compares each school to other, similar schools is perhaps the most valuable. Data provided by the DCSF, QCDA and OfSTED is helpful, but must obviously be treated with caution as to whether the performance of each school/department is statistically different from that of other schools with similar catchments, whether the school context is affecting performance, or whether the data reveals underachievement or value added.

Much of the insistence on achieving targets has a positive impact on education. Who could disagree with the intention of both encouraging and supporting students in doing their best? However, just as teachers cannot learn for their students, so they also cannot achieve targets for them – it is therefore essential to enable students to become responsible, autonomous and independent in their learning. Teachers can identify gaps, suggest targets and provide methods to reach them, but the students themselves have to take responsibility for their own improvement (Butt 2006d).

8 | Equality of opportunity in assessment – the case of boys' underachievement

The educational provision made for children in Britain's schools is uneven. Where there is an obvious inequality of provision – between state schooling for 'all', but selective independent and private schooling for a privileged, wealthy few – then questions of fairness of educational outcomes will always arise. One of the perennial debates about British schooling concerns whether its assessment regime rewards student achievement fairly. These issues are clearly revealed by the generally better performance in examinations of students attending non-state schools. Children do not all share an equality of opportunity to access what are (arguably) each nation's best schools – whose status and performance are often enhanced by the nature of their financial income, the social and economic standing of the parents who send their children to these schools, the schools' traditions, and a variety of other factors both seen and unseen. Having made this point, let us focus on some of the evidence for inequity in assessment outcomes in state schools.

Consider the assessed performance of the population of students aged 4 to 19 within state schools in England and Wales. Using any assessment measures – be they SATs, GCSEs, A and AS levels, teacher-assessed levels in the National Curriculum, Diplomas, or vocational qualifications results – certain trends in student performance exist which reveal inequities. First, boys and girls perform and achieve differently in examinations. Second, assessed performance varies by ethnic grouping. Third, social economic status has a marked impact on achievement. Fourth, the educational background of parents has a significant influence on the attainment of their offspring. This short, crudely stated list could be extended further, although it is probably more important to consider whether assessment simply reveals these inequities, or whether it has a part to play in *creating* them. This chapter uses the first of these examples of differences in students' assessed performance – boys' underachievement – as a lens through which to consider equality of opportunity in assessment.

Some reasons for inequity in assessment outcomes

Consider the following, which may give rise to variations in the assessed performance of students:

◆ *Curriculum content taught:* Does the curriculum motivate and appeal to all children in the same ways? Are particular individuals and/or groups (ethnic, social, economic, etc.) more motivated by particular content and therefore more likely to perform better when assessed?

◆ *Type of teaching experienced:* Which students have their preferred learning styles catered for? Does this affect their attainment and subsequent performance in assessments?

◆ *Assessment methods used:* Are these biased towards one group of learners or another?

◆ *Performance expectations:* Do (certain) teachers and students have particularly high or low expectations of assessment outcomes? Does this have an impact on their motivation to perform well? Does the performance of some students reveal self-fulfilling prophecies regarding their previous learning?

◆ *Feedback:* Does the assessment feedback provided by the teacher/assessor lead to the motivation or disillusionment of students?

Teachers and schools strive to minimize the negative impact of many of the issues highlighted above, but in so doing may face some thorny ethical questions. For example, is it right to change teaching and assessment methods in an attempt to raise the performance levels of one group, if this may have a negative impact on the performance of another? If we know that boys tend to outperform girls when completing decision-making exercises, should we extend their use to help raise boys' performance? Or, if we know that girls are better than boys at long-term project work, should we avoid using this as a means of assessment in an effort to equalize differences in performance between the sexes? Surely the 'right' approach is to try to balance the methods of assessment used, such that each are included within the learning experience but not to such an extent that one group gains advantage simply by virtue of the means of assessment employed.

Underachievement versus low achievement

Emma Smith (2005, 2008) focuses our attention on what we understand by the term 'underachievement' – which is widely used in education, but with little apparent consensus. She highlights that underachievement has many causes, both within and beyond schools, each of which need to be considered if we are to close the achievement gap between students. The use of examination performance data, nationally and internationally, has led to:

> ... many countries re-examining their education systems in light of perceived failings in these comparative assessments ... In the UK, unfavourable international comparisons have contributed to the assertion that the performance of certain groups of students is characterised by a 'long tail' of underachievement and government policy has its focus firmly on raising standards and eliminating all forms of underachievement. (Smith 2008, p. 6)

In part, this explains our obsession with large-scale collection and analysis of assessment data. Despite the long-standing disparity between the achievement of students from different socio-economic backgrounds, most recent national assessment data appears to suggest that the achievement of all students is improving and that the persistent gap between boys' and girls' performance is actually narrowing.

But what is 'underachievement', and how does it differ from 'low achievement'? The notion of underachievement relies on our first having an expectation of what a realistic level of achievement for each child, or for particular groups of children, should be (Gorard and Smith 2004). Often the casual labelling of students, such as 'underachieving boys', does little to help – for this surely does not mean that *all* boys underachieve, compared to girls? But then which group(s) of boys, with which characteristics, should we target as underachievers? Or do we actually mean 'low achievers' – students who perform below the norm, but whose work and attainment are acceptable and understandable given their innate level of ability and circumstances? This is different from underachievement, for many low achievers work exceptionally hard but may still obtain only modest results. A very able child who is not interested in a piece of academic work may perform well compared to his or her peers, but below their usual high level of performance. This child must surely be 'underachieving', rather than being labelled as a 'low achiever'. The reasons behind persistent or sporadic underachievement are, needless to say, complex. There is a myriad of social, academic, personal and behavioural reasons why some children underachieve. What is perhaps most important is to identify the reasons for persistent underachievement – which has led to the labelling of, say, 'underachieving boys' and the recognition of underachievement among certain ethnic and socio-economic groups. Significantly, in most countries, the largest achievement gaps are seen between children from different income groups. This division is much larger and more persistent than that which exists between the achievement of boys and girls (Smith 2008).

Who are the underachievers?

Much has been made of boys' underachievement over the past few years, although we know that various groups of girls also under-achieve (see Bradley Smith 2002, Butt 2001, Francis 2000). Across all the phases of education the gap between boys' and girls' achievement is widest in the language-based subjects and narrowest in Mathematics and the sciences. Particularly at GCSE level, girls' performance outstrips that of boys', although in recent years the gap has gradually closed and the rate of improvement made by boys is now higher than that of girls: 'the proportion of boys achieving grade C or above in English increased by nearly 20 per cent between 1996 and 2007, compared with around 10 per cent for girls' (Smith 2008, p. 7). However, boys' underachievement is still evidenced in national statistics for almost all examination subjects. Big questions are therefore raised about why boys continue to underperform – is it to do with different motivation, or different ability? Are boys not so interested in learning, or are they just not as 'bright' as girls? Are they poorly organized, or more immature? Is the variation in assessed performance closely correlated with the types of assessment used? Do boys perform better on short, factual tests and girls on longer, extended pieces of writing, or coursework? Which are the most fair and equitable assessment methods to use so as not to unfairly advantage one sex over another? Or, more tantalizingly, is it a combination of these factors? (Bleach 2000).

The case of boys' underachievement is not unique to English and Welsh schools. Similar trends are seen in other developed countries (see Foster *et al.* 2001 for a perspective on boys' underachievement in the UK, Australia and the USA). The Programme for International Student Assessment (PISA), which facilitates international comparisons of student achievements through common testing, also reveals boys' underachievement. Such comparative results have encouraged the UK government to target underachievement and the raising of standards through policies and initiatives which increase testing and target-setting. Boys' underachievement has also stimulated a debate which has polarized into considerations of whether they are being 'failed' by the education and assessment system, or by the innate characteristics of their sex (Epstein *et al.* 1998). To the general public such underachievement is often linked to student disaffection, disruptive behaviour and the increased likelihood of exclusion from school (Butt *et al.* 2004).

Jackson (2003) categorizes research into boys' underachievement into four main areas:

1. The nature and size of the gender gap (e.g. Gorard *et al.* 1999, Warrington and Younger 1999).
2. Differences in attainment of the genders (e.g Arnot *et al.* 1998, Gillborn and Mirza 2000).
3. The nature of the public debate about boys' achievements (e.g. Delamont 1999, Epstein *et al.* 1998, Younger *et al.* 1999).
4. Strategies for raising boys' attainment (Jackson 2002, Sukhnandan *et al.* 2000, cited in Butt *et al.* 2004).

The main socio-cultural reasons advanced for boys' underachievement is the cult of 'laddishness' that often impedes their academic progress. Such behaviour protects boys from harsh judgement by their peers for poor academic performance, or avoids them being labelled as exhibiting 'feminine' traits associated with academic work (Jackson 2002, 2003; Martino 1999). The desire to appear cool, popular, laid back and not bothered by academic success is linked to a culture of wanting to be seen to apply oneself in school. For many boys the goal is to appear effortless in their achievement – 'a characteristic that boys see as a masculine trait, unsullied by the feminine indignity of having to work hard for one's successes' (Butt *et al.* 2004, p. 332). Interestingly, parallel connections have been made with the behaviour of some male black students in North American schools, who underperform to avoid being labelled as 'white' by their peers. Success in assessment, which is strongly linked to notions of achievement, is often publicly displayed through the awarding of marks and grades – many boys seek to protect their self-worth by avoiding the possibilities of being labelled as failures, either by ostentatious lack of effort, procrastination, refusing to complete academic work, disruption, or disinterest – all 'acceptable' excuses for failure among their peer group. For many boys this appears preferable to striving and failing, or admitting one's lack of ability (Butt *et al.* 2004). The feminization of the teaching workforce has also been raised as a possible cause of boys' underachievement. The plethora of short-term government initiatives to improve boys' underachievement – often tentative in nature and relying on self-help 'toolkits' for teachers and students – has not yet solved the root problems. Little help has been given to teachers in identifying why problems occur, and scant attention to whether it is the subjects themselves, the means of assessment, pedagogy, various issues related to gender or a combination of all these factors which account for boys' underachievement (see Butt *et al.* 2004, 2006). There is a need for more evidence-based guidance on the importance of assessment in supporting learning, such as Molly Warrington and Mike Younger's Raising Boys' Achievement Project – a long-term research project tasked to investigate and identify strategies which have sustained effects on raising boys' achievement.

Some of what has been discovered, which begins to answer why the standards of certain boys' achievements are modest compared to girls, is captured below:

> One finding that appears clear is that many boys perform poorly on tasks that are completed over a series of lessons or homeworks, rather than within a shorter, more discrete timeframe. This may explain the tendency for boys to do badly at coursework, but better on shorter writing tasks performed under examination conditions or within single lessons. There is also evidence that many boys feel that applying their knowledge and understanding within a written context loses the immediacy of oral response, often merely involving a repetition of what has already been 'completed' successfully in class. Girls appear less

willing to become involved in 'competitive' oral question and answer and whole-class discussion work in lessons, preferring to demonstrate their ability through their writing. This allows them greater opportunity for reflection and expression. It therefore seems likely that if boys are unable to work, or to be assessed, in the ways *they* prefer, this will affect their performance more dramatically than girls. (Butt *et al.* 2004, p. 343)

Boys who underperform often display similar socio-cultural and socio-economic characteristics, relating in particular to their class, ethnicity and the level of their parents' education. The higher achievement of girls across the Key Stages and at GCSE often narrows considerably at AS and A level, and may even reverse in some subjects as they progress into higher education. Why this gender gap narrows is interesting. Evidence suggests this is partly through self-selection, with only the higher achieving boys progressing, through changes in student motivation, alteration in teaching methods, and a shift in learning and assessment styles. But each student's case is different, with every child having subtly nuanced reasons for the variations in their assessed performance. Despite the narrowing gap, Bekhradnia (2009) warns about complacency regarding differences in male and female performance in higher education, noting that 'on all measures of achievement the difference that begins in school continues into and through university' (p. 27).

What can we do to raise the standards of boys' achievement? There appear to be a number of characteristics common to the schools in which boys perform well. These schools have a good sense of community, have worked hard to break down any 'macho' male culture, and provide positive male role models. They value achievement and respond quickly to students' work, providing detailed and constructive feedback. Warrington and Younger's research on the Raising Boys' Achievement Project suggests that strategies for addressing boys' underachievement are grouped into four categories:

1   *Organizational* – schools having a clear ethos of equality of opportunity, culture of achievement, high expectations, reward and praise, self-esteem, encouraging responsibility.
2   *Individual* – using assessment data for target-setting for students, allowing early identification of children performing at a lower level than expected.

3   *Pedagogic* – specific initiatives to develop boys' writing, clarifying lesson aims, objectives and assessment criteria.

4   *Socio-cultural* – attempting to change images of 'laddish' masculinity to portray learning as acceptable for boys, behaviour management schemes, working with parents, using male role models, and using 'key' students to support strategies so that others follow. (Cited in Butt *et al.* 2004)

Interesting moral and ethical questions arise: even if research succeeded in discovering the reasons why boys and girls achieve differently, would we necessarily want to act on its findings (Wood 2002)? For example, if it were proven that teaching girls and boys in single-sex groups improved their attainment, would we want to do this for their entire school careers? Are there bigger social advantages to co-educational learning that outweigh the possible academic advantages? If we discovered that a certain teaching method (or mode of assessment) significantly improved the achievement of boys, would we condone its use if this discriminated against girls' performance? If it was proved that boys respond best to being taught by male teachers, would we want to, indeed could we, change our teaching arrangements to accommodate this? In essence, should we strive to maximize academic performance, disregarding the social impacts of doing so? Research findings always need to be interpreted and may form only one strand of our decision-making.

Conclusions

The question of how the gap between high and low achievers should be narrowed, both within and between the sexes, is a difficult one. A myriad of solutions has been tried: 'High-stakes testing, formative assessment and single-sex groupings in mixed-sex schools, to list only a few, have all been embraced by governments who are keen to promote evidence-based practices to raise standards' (Smith 2008, p. 8). However, despite a plethora of initiatives and research projects, both large and small, we are still only slightly closer to finding out 'what works' in terms of raising (some) boys' achievement. The reasons for this are easily stated – achievement is influenced and mediated by agents far beyond the classroom, for the determinants underpinning student performance and achievement are deeply rooted in societal factors beyond the direct control of schools. Assessment data is only a signifier of a problem – it is not, in itself, neces-sarily the source of the solution. Perhaps the whole differential achievement issue needs to be more clearly defined – what *are* the problems we are trying to solve? Is our aim to narrow the overall achievement gap, bringing the performance and attainment of low and high achievers closer together? Or is this less important than targeting the performance of low achievers? Or underachievers? Or a particular group (or groups) of one, or the other? At present, the evidence for successful intervention is largely limited, and often con-tradictory. Smith (2008) even goes so far as to question our continued use of the term 'underachievement', referring to it as: 'a concept over which there is much confusion and little consensus. It is a term that has probably outlived its usefulness' (p. 8).

The fact that the assessment gap between boys and girls persists into higher education, where girls' participation is currently much closer to the government's target of 50 per cent (at 49.2 per cent) than boys (at only 37.8 per cent), is worrying. Bekhradnia (2009) notes that in most subjects women outnumber men, and that 'the relatively poor performance of men occurs throughout society; it's true of middle-class as well as of working-class males and it occurs in all ethnic groups' (p. 27) – a problem which he believes is exacerbated in England and Wales by the GCSE examination system and the teaching associated with it (see also Asthana 2009). The correlation between the year in which GCSEs were introduced and when boys' performance started to lag behind that of girls Bekhradnia believes is not coincidental.

9 | Making assessment easier? The role of e-assessment

This chapter provides a perspective on the use of ICT to assist assessment in schools, offering a commentary on the main issues surrounding the introduction of electronic assessment, or e-assessment. A variety of definitions of the term 'e-assessment' exists, although the following is arguably one of the most serviceable: 'the use of electronic processes for registration of candidates to certification and also the end-to-end assessment processes from the perspective of learners, practitioners, school administrators, learning establishments, awarding bodies and members of the general public' (JISC/QCA 2006). The term 'e-assessment' has arisen to describe a range of assessment activities, sometimes referred to as Computer Based Assessment (CBA), Computer Assisted Assessment (CAA), or Computer Moderated Assessment (CMA) – terms that reflect the extent to which computers are intrinsic or extrinsic to both the setting and assessment of tasks. The potential of technology to assist in assessment is considerable, while the speed at which technological change is affecting all aspects of our lives suggests that teachers will soon need to become competent users of e-assessment. Examination Awarding Bodies are already utilizing online delivery and marking technologies for high stakes public examinations, while on-screen testing – using materials from previous, paper-based tests – has also been successfully trialled. Examination scripts have also been marked online, with candidates' work having been scanned and sent electronically to examiners for assessment (Rynne 2009). Here the logistical advantages of e-assessment over traditional postage-based examination systems are considerable: e-assessment avoids the necessity for large volumes of examination papers and scripts to be securely packaged, sent and monitored between the Awarding Body, the school and the examiner. Many aspects of e-assessment practices will inevitably filter down into schools – not only will e-assessment alter large-scale, high stakes, national assessment processes, but also the assessment of students' day-to-day work produced in the classroom or at home.

For some time the British government has considered that schools have not used technology in the most effective ways possible to advance learning, improve management, support assessment and alleviate problems of staff workload (Butt and Gunter 2007). The willingness of the Department for Children, Families and Schools (DCSF), and its predecessor the DfES, to invest in ICT–based solutions to help modernize educational practice has been considerable. This enthusiasm has embraced assessment, where the potential for e-assessment to act as a catalyst for educational change, to modernize assessment practices and to deliver government policies has been noted. However, the government's direction of change has not always been clear: for example, in 2006 the DfES disbanded its Technology Directorate, leading to questions about national policy leadership on e-assessment, while in 2005 the QCA wound up its recently formed e-strategy unit (see Ripley 2007). During this period the QCA also published two reviews of the use of ICT in assessment, both of which stressed overwhelmingly negative aspects of the application of technology – the first review focused on e-plagiarism (linked to the government's desire to reduce coursework in public examinations), while the second reported on the increasing use of digital devices to cheat in examinations (Ripley 2007). The tension between the QCA's role in championing government strategy for technology use in learning and assessment, its responsibility to regulate and control assessment practices, and its desire to maintain public confidence in the security of the examination system, is palpable.

In 2005 the DfES launched a challenging education e-strategy, 'Harnessing Technology: Transforming learning and children's services', designed to encompass all educational stakeholders, informing them about how technology could be used to transform many aspects of education (DfES, 2005). In terms of assessment this heralded the greater use of technology to support existing paper-based testing, as well as the implementation of online, on demand, assessment systems. Arguably the responsibility to maintain the cutting edge of innovation in national e-assessment sits within the QCDA, which in 2005 published a blueprint (effectively a five-year plan) for the future of e-assessment (Figure 9.1).

- ◆ All new qualifications should include assessment on-screen.
- ◆ Awarding bodies set up to accept and assess e-portfolios.
- ◆ Most examinations should be available optionally on-screen, where appropriate.
- ◆ National Curriculum tests available on-screen for those schools that want to use them.
- ◆ The first on-demand GCSE examinations are starting to be introduced.
- ◆ Ten new qualifications specifically designed for electronic delivery and assessment (source http://www.qca.org.uk).

Figure 9.1: A proposed blueprint for delivering e-assessment

There is now optimism about the extent to which technology can advance both pedagogical and assessment practices in schools (Butt and Gunter 2007). This is expressed through the belief that digital tools can transform the ways in which students learn and how they are subsequently assessed. However, teachers and governments alike may need to be more critically aware of the limitations, as well as the potential strengths, of using technology for assessment purposes. John (2005) has argued that school subject cultures tend to be built on deep traditions which need to be understood if the use of technology is to become successfully embedded into curricular and assessment practices. He particularly focuses on the need for policy-makers and innovators – who, he believes, tend to think in revolutionary rather than evolutionary terms – to consider how their expectations might mesh with teacher pragmatism. The pace of change in e-assessment will almost certainly not be as rapid as some hope. Indeed, one survey revealed that, by 2007, only some 15 per cent of schools in England had embedded technology appropriately into their teaching and learning practices (Ripley 2008). By extension, this would suggest that the use of e-assessment in English schools is currently modest (Butt and Gunter 2007).

One of the most important factors to consider is the process of teacher adoption of technology-based innovation. As John (2005) asserts, when teachers seek to extend their personal use of ICT, even under well-supported conditions, they often take substantial amounts of time to accommodate new technologies into their teaching, learning and assessment. He believes that a new blending of 'technology and subject' has to take place which, for many teachers, highlights the necessity of achieving a 'pragmatic pedagogy'. Initial resistance to the use of technology among many teachers can be high – Olson (2000), for example, questions why teachers would want to move from the safety of their existing teaching methods towards the uncertainty of technology-based teaching and assessment. Teachers also embrace and assimilate ICT according to a complex mix of factors – subject culture, personal professional histories, previous experience of using technology, and the extent of technical support available are all important in teachers' adoption of e-assessment.

The inevitable growth of e-assessment

The Joint Information Systems Committee (JISC) has suggested that a number of 'drivers and influencers' exist in the adoption and development of e-assessment (Figure 9.2):

There are three main areas that both impact on and are affected by e-assessment

Institutional
– strategic, cultural and operational

Technical
– infrastructure, delivery, security
– content design, presentation, item bank use
– standards, interoperability, accessibility

Pedagogical
– new opportunities for learning and teaching

Other key activities that impact on e-assessment
– developments in e-portfolios, short-term/lifelong records
– JISC partnership with Becta to provide a cohesive approach to e-assessment and e-portfolios for schools, post-16 and HE.
(JISC 2006)

Figure 9.2 Impact drivers and influencers

ICT is already used in numerous ways in schools, both inside and beyond the classroom, providing a platform for further innovation. It has been argued that technology is capable of addressing all the aspects of learning and assessment traditionally undertaken by the teacher or examiner. Electronic forms of monitoring, assessing, recording, reporting and accountability are all available through e-assessment, with supporters claiming that technology can now improve on traditional practices. E-assessment can be used to set questions and tasks, collect student responses, store and distribute students' work, facilitate marking and ease reporting. Marking can be conducted online either by humans, computers or a combination of both. The sophistication of online testing is rapidly advancing, moving away from the use of simple multiple-choice tests to the assessment of more sophisticated problem-solving and decision-making exercises. However, stakeholders must be convinced of the potential of e-assessment to add value to current practice: e-assess-ment should be faster, more efficient, more flexible and at least as rigorous as previous pencil and paper assessment methods. In an era of individualized learning, e-assessment must also provide the capability for young people to control and direct their learning and assessment. If e-assessment can deliver on its promises its future is assured. Recent curriculum changes, such as the introduction of Diplomas and 14–19 reforms, have highlighted the necessity to broaden our assessment procedures. These have particularly focused on the introduction of extended projects, where the learning and assessment framework is well suited to the students' use of technol-ogy to compile text, create presentations, use DVDs and videos, gather photographs and create CD-Roms.

What are the advantages of e-assessment?

The advantages of e-assessment must surely relate to what electronic systems can do that conventional, traditional, paper-based systems cannot. The introduction of questions and tasks which use multi-media materials is a major strength, proving that for certain activities e-assessment can be much more flexible than previous 'pencil and paper' tests. The possibilities of creating links to e-learning facilities that integrate teaching and learning resources with various forms of assessment are strong. Here, e-assessment, which is still a novel expe-rience for most students, can prove to be motivational and engaging.

Certainly the possibilities of creating assessments that respond, or adapt, to the students' answers – either providing prompts and hints to support them, or offering various routes to enable the student to achieve a solution to a problem – give an interactive edge that traditional forms of assessment find difficult to simulate. The facility to individualize tests or assessments may also be valuable, generating tasks that are closely geared to the needs of the particular child. The learning and assessment possibilities are considerable, involving:

> Interactive displays which show change in variables over time, microworlds and simulations, interfaces that present complex data in ways that are easy to control, all facilitate the assessment of problem-solving and process skills such as understanding and representing problems, controlling variables, generating and testing hypotheses, and finding rules and relationships. (Ridgway, McCusker and Read, 2004)

In many respects, the main advantages of e-assessment relate to its organizational qualities, rather than its innovation of assessment materials. E-assessment offers the possibilities for rapid, large-scale distribution of assessment tasks to numerous 'centres', or individuals, at the press of a button. Encryption will ensure that this process is secure, within acceptable limits. Significant advantages will also occur through the ability of e-assessment systems not only to store and distribute assessment materials, but also to gather and co-ordinate marking and the distribution of awards. Although not directly linked to the improvement of classroom practice and learning, automated delivery and retrieval systems may help in the management of assessment data in schools, as well as in the storage of assessment instruments. Banks of assessment items could be stored centrally, accessible online, to enable teachers to access them at any time for use with their students. Once marking has been completed the results could be distributed electronically, data sets analysed, and central record systems co-ordinated with different levels of access afforded to teachers, students and other stakeholders. Theoretically this should speed assessment practice and might even be developed so that candidates could receive rapid, individualized feedback on their electronically marked assessments. Centralized analysis of performance might also be provided to teachers, students and others following the collation and analysis of assessment data.

The potential benefits of e-assessment can therefore be summarized as follows:

◆ Positive effect on student motivation and performance.
◆ Freeing of teachers' time, particularly through the supply of quality assessments, auto-marking and the creation of time to focus on analysing and interpreting results.
◆ High quality assessment resources, available electronically online, on CD-Rom/DVD or via websites.
◆ Provision of diagnostic information, such as reports for candidates that outline specific areas for further study, or for teachers highlighting students whose progress is at risk.
◆ Flexibility and ease of use; provision of tests when the learner is ready and on demand. Diagnostic testing can also be provided at the most appropriate time.
◆ Linking learning and assessment; providing the learning with formative information and empowering them to make the next steps. E-portfolios enable students to collect assessment information, reflect and analyse the data, and make (supported) decisions about their next educational steps.
◆ Assessment of higher order thinking skills, such as decision-making and problem-solving skills.
◆ Inevitability; on-screen assessment in many professional jobs is already here, while awarding bodies are introducing e-assessment in public examinations. (After Ripley 2008)

Developing e-assessment in schools

The development of ICT systems has progressed to the extent that most schools now operate some form of virtual learning environment (VLE) to support their teaching, learning and assessment. One of the challenges that schools have grappled with has involved making their VLE accessible to students off-site, such that assessment tasks can be accessed, completed and submitted remotely outside school hours. Because not all students currently have access to broadband outside school – something the UK government has promised to address by 2012 – this currently creates equality of opportunity issues. Allowing students access to school-based systems at break and lunchtime, or after school, does not maximize the potential of e-assessment.

VLE system managers and senior management teams in schools need to consider the range of materials that they will make available to staff and students via their networks. In the field of e-assessment numerous commercial organizations produce assessment materials which, like any educational resources, have to be carefully scrutinized for their educational value. Many assessment software packages offer multiple-choice testing, 'drag and drop' exercises, and auto-marked tests which provide instant feedback to the student (Rynne 2009). However, these assessment activities have their own validity, reliability and fitness for purpose issues which need careful consideration by teachers; there may also be issues of compatability of commercial software with the particular VLE of the school. Additionally, many students are sophisticated users of technology who have high expectations of both the production qualities and capabilities of commercial software packages – meeting the expectations of students in this regard obviously comes at a price.

One of the major advantages of e-assessment is its flexibility. For example, teachers can establish different forms of assessment online, such that students gain access to these at whatever point the teacher or student wants. This can be tailored so that student access is offered under particular conditions – when the teacher is available for face-to-face consultation, at a point in learning when it is most convenient to release the assessment exercises, in different forms of task according to the students' strengths and needs, or on demand at any time. The potential to individualize assessment tasks which particular students have access to, or to randomly generate questions on a topic from a 'question bank', is also powerful. Some VLEs give teachers the opportunity to monitor the students' efforts as they work, making their computer screens visible as thumbnails on a teacher's monitor (Rynne 2009). This gives the teacher an opportunity to check on individual and class progress, so that he or she can offer additional instruction and guidance, or display examples of students' work to support the learning of others. The opportunity to facilitate class, peer and self-assessment is therefore considerable, promoting aspects of assessment for learning. E-assessment can therefore be utilized to increase student responsibility and autonomy in their learning and assessment, offering them the chance to manage their assessed work. Here the practice of submitting work to a file or folder, accessible by both student and teacher, develops organizational and management skills. Despite the fact that computer systems have their own unique ways of either corrupting or losing students' work, with practice the collection, marking, archiving and distribution of work will steadily become more efficient and commonplace.

Hand-held interactive devices, which students can use to register their answers to questions posed in classrooms or lecture halls – similar to gameshows which have an 'ask the audience' component – can invigorate assessment for learning. Here the teacher can instantly survey the students' responses to particular questions, using this information to gauge how secure the class is in its understanding. All students, not just those who usually gain the teacher's attention, have an opportunity to feed back on their understanding of what is being taught. This process places the student at the heart of the process of learning and assessment, prompting Ripley (2007) to comment that handheld interactive devices could constitute a radical driver for change in classroom assessment practice. A fixed range of responses, chosen simultaneously and collated electronically, can provide an almost instantaneous analysis of the students' knowledge and understanding, which can either be presented as a pie chart or a percentage to facilitate rapid assessment feedback. The interactive and motivational nature of such activities is key – all students are engaged, meaning that no individuals or groups can dominate the assessment process.

Personal Desktop Assistants (PDAs) have also been employed in teaching, learning and assessment. Students have utilized this technology to complete assessed tasks such as decision-making exercises and enquiry projects, harnessing the PDAs' capabilities to enable photographing, videoing, voice recording, note taking and sketching. PDAs have been used by individual students and within groups, with portfolios of work eventually being loaded onto a website for marking. Other projects have engaged students in virtual worlds, similar to Second Life where players adopt the roles of avatars, in which they are tasked to solve problems and undertake activities which are then assessed. Interestingly Ridgway, McCusker and Read (2004) comment on the dislocation between the use of such technology in learning situations and its restricted use for assessment purposes: 'currently we have bizarre assessment practices where students use ICT tools such as word processors and graphics calculators as an integral part of learning, and are then restricted to paper and pencil when their "knowledge" is assessed' (p. 4).

What's next in e-assessment?

A variety of new developments in e-assessment will soon be introduced to schools, as explained by Rynne (2009):

◆ Computerized adaptive testing, where questions are drawn randomly from a question bank categorized according to degree of difficulty. When students succeed at one level the next question is drawn from the question bank at a higher level, and so on. If they get the question wrong then the selection of the next question drops back to the level below. This continues until a point is reached where students' responses stabilize at a particular level. This requires a huge bank of questions where the degree of difficulty is clearly established.

◆ E-assessments, whereby each student's response to each question is recorded, and those who show some understanding but not full mastery are distinguished from those who are able to respond correctly without further support. Students' errors are analysed, and guidance is given relating to the nature of the misunderstanding which underlies each common mistake. Teaching activities are suggested to develop students' deeper understanding of the concepts which the assessment indicates they find difficult. Thus the circle is closed, and the outcome of the formative assessment feeds directly into the next steps for teaching and learning for each individual student.

◆ Digital Capture Pens, which store students' answers electronically and can include peer assessments on the same page. (After Rynne 2009, pp. 44–5)

Undoubtedly, in such a rapidly changing area of assessment practice, new e-assessment products will continue to surface on an almost daily basis. The challenge is to ensure that these are used in ways which meet the underlying principles of validity, reliability and fitness for purpose we would wish to see in all our assessment practices.

E-portfolios

E-portfolios offer the prospect of learning and assessment being closely integrated. Here the expectation is the provision of a complete package of individualized support and guidance for learners, alongside ways of recording and monitoring process, while encouraging the learner to become more autonomous and self-directed. The scope is ambitious, with 'Harnessing Technology' (DfES 2005) envisaging that e-portfolios will be accessible through secure links by students, teachers, parents and other stakeholders across all educational sectors and relevant public and private organizations. With greater flexibility for modern learners to learn how, where and when they wish, Ripley (2008) envisages that we will require 'assessment systems (to be) able to follow the learner and accredit a wide range of evidence of learning. E-portfolios and e-assessment have a fundamental role to play in joining learning with assessment and enabling the learner to monitor progress' (p. 161).

Similar to conventional assessment portfolios (see Chapter 6), e-portfolios will serve as repositories of records of learning, assessments, exemplar student work and records of other achievements and activities. E-portfolios could also enhance the way in which these records are presented to various audiences, and be used to encourage individualized planning and progression, or to illustrate areas of strength and areas for development. Just as with paper-based portfolios and records of achievement, the e-portfolio could support students as they progress from one educational institution or course to another.

Conclusions

The title of this chapter questions whether e-assessment will make assessment easier. Given that e-assessment is still in its infancy it is not possible to provide a definitive answer, although the potential gains are becoming clearer. At its most simplistic, e-assessment merely replicates what we currently do through pencil and paper tests – for example, by providing conventional tasks online to be downloaded and applied in the traditional manner. Such practice misses a huge opportunity to radically shift the acts of learning and assessment. At its most advanced, e-assessment can promote the principles of formative assessment – the vision being to enable students to become more autonomous and reflective learners, who make responsible choices about when, where and how they will be assessed. With teacher support, students could be assessed almost 'on demand' through flexible assessment formats which will be geared to diagnose problems, set targets and promote learning. E-assessment therefore has the power to motivate learners to change their approaches to education within and beyond the classroom. The principles of valid, reliable assessment, which is fit for purpose, must overlay e-assessment innovations – we must still remember that it is essential to assess what is important to learn, not what is easiest to assess.

It is easy to be dazzled by what technology claims it can do. We must ensure that e-assessment fulfils its promise to improve our assessment practices – either by accelerating the assessment process, by adding value to current procedures, by doing something we could not do before, or by improving efficiency and effectiveness. In a society where expectations of greater individuality and personal-ization of service grow daily, e-assessment appears well placed to meet some of these needs by providing assessment and feedback 'on demand'. The effects will be dramatic, although not necessarily always positive, as expectations will sometimes be raised beyond the capabilities of people or technology to deliver. In our public exami-nations, which are continually under close scrutiny, e-assessment must be introduced with care if the whole assessment system is not to be accused of lowering standards, rejecting comparability and 'dumbing down' (Boston 2005).

A number of significantly sized hurdles therefore need to be crossed before it can be claimed that e-assessment makes our assess-ment lives easier – many subjects have a sub-culture which provides resistance to the use of ICT, often related to a lack of awareness of what the technology can do. Receiving appropriate training in the use of hardware and software is still a major issue for many teachers – with around 50 per cent of teachers reporting that they have not received the training necessary to use ICT competently, and most teachers having learned how to use technology informally through contact with other teachers who have greater competence, knowl-edge or understanding of its use (Butt and Gunter 2007). Perhaps one of the biggest hurdles is the investment of additional time and effort that using ICT implies for the classroom practitioner. Many departments still lack easy access to computers in school, while not all students are online at home. The potential, and the expectation, of e-assessment is high. Hopefully it will in future act as 'a stimulus for rethinking the whole curriculum, as well as all current assessment systems' (Ridgway, McCusker and Read 2004).

10 | Making assessment matter

We can recognize the power that assessment has either to support, or to hinder, teaching and learning – for it exerts a profound influence on what is taught, what is learned and on who succeeds in education. It is important to acknowledge the huge impact that assessment outcomes have on an individual's learning career, their motivation to engage with educational processes and on their opportunities in life. Indeed, for many young people, high stakes assessments publicly determine who among them will be considered educationally worthy, and who will fall by the wayside. In this context the comparatively recent focus on Assessment for Learning in British schools – an expression of our growing realization of the importance of formative assessment to the act of learning – has not occurred by chance. We now realize that getting assessment practices right can mean the difference between teaching children who are motivated and rewarded by their schooling, or dealing with the consequences of those students who struggle to cope with the negative labelling that is so often associated with assessment regimes.

Assessment should always place the child at the heart of the education process. It would be foolish to deny the importance of summative assessment, league tables, analysis of assessment data, 'levering up' of standards and the drive for school improvement – all of which draw significantly on the use of assessment data. But the *real* foundations of educational success should not be forgotten. Instilling in children a love of learning, out of which grows both confidence and autonomy, should surely be the main aim of education. Assessment plays a vital role in the learning process, arguably greater than the influence of either subject content or pedagogical approach, but it should do nothing to damage the goal of advancing children's learning (Harlen 2008b). Children themselves make stern judgements about their abilities as learners from an early age, and we need to be aware of how easily this is further reinforced by our assessment of their performance in school work. Handled badly, such judgements can lead to stress, disengagement and 'learned helplessness' where students no longer take appropriate educational risks, but strive for constant teacher support and reassurance to help them achieve the 'right answer'. Where children are unsure of their educational goals – conflating the significance of achieving a good mark for an assessed *product*, with the greater importance of understanding a key learning *process* – then assessment has overstepped the mark. Encouraging learners to become constructively self-critical, reflective individuals, capable of self- and peer assessment, puts assessment back in its rightful place. The key is communication: the teacher supporting the learner with regard to why they are learning a particular topic, how this learning will be assessed, what criteria exist for measuring success and how to meet those criteria. Understanding why achievement has (or has not) occurred is important, as this forms the first step towards meaningful target-setting and target-getting.

Achieving high-quality assessment in the classroom is not easy. It requires of the teacher a delicate mix of personal and professional judgement, competence, skill and confidence in the use of a range of assessment techniques. Successful classroom assessment is dynamic – it cannot stand still, for teachers constantly need to re-visit their previous judgements of students' abilities and performance, while realizing the motivational (or de-motivational) effects of the assessment methods they use. There is no such thing as an infallible, teacher-proof, objective, assessment instrument. Similarly, the results of assessments are also imperfect, requiring interpretation if their true significance is to be realized. We must be realistic about what assessment can, and cannot do, as well as recognizing the distinct possibilities of user error.

The education systems in economically developed countries could not function without assessment. We must strive to eradicate, reduce or ameliorate those assessment practices that are potentially damaging to the learner, while promoting forms of assessment that help students to learn. Assessment is all about measurement and making judgements: it is therefore a very powerful tool which must be handled carefully. We have seen that at best assessment can motivate, encourage and shape us as learners; at worst it reduces us to being little more than depersonalized data.

The relationship between teaching, learning, attainment and performance is neither simple, linear nor straightforward (Black and Wiliam 2008c). Over-reliance on one form of testing to ascertain student performance and attainment is fraught with dangers. Better to have confidence in a set of well-reasoned principles and practices as the foundation for assessment methods, than to place all of one's assessment eggs in one basket. We should be more cautious about what assessment can do, and question whether its claims are legitimate – particularly when these are (supposedly) neutral, value-free and objective.

Why is day-to-day teacher assessment often weak?

In this concluding chapter it is worth reminding ourselves of the main issues currently associated with assessment practices in schools. According to recent OfSTED school inspection reports of both primary and secondary schools, and a report specifically targeting assessment practice at secondary level (OfSTED 2003), one of the perennially weakest areas of teachers' professional practice remains the day-to-day assessment of students' work. It is clear that many teachers have maintained the same assessment practices for years, hardly varying their approach – a situation which may lead to a number of questionable assessment habits developing. These teachers tend not to employ methods of assessment that are formative, educationally supportive and student-centred. As such, much of their commonly used classroom-based assessment is of limited educational use to students, while some is positively damaging to their learning (Butt 2006e).

This book has attempted to champion the use of formative assessment, as well as supporting the development of students' abilities to self-assess and picture the next stages of their learning in terms of what they need to do to perform better. Unfortunately, the daily assessment practices used in many classrooms may still do little to promote this approach. The following is a list of eight points, originally prompted by the work of Black and Wiliam (1998b) and further explored by Butt (2006e), that need addressing if assessment in schools is to improve. These were noted, briefly, in the introductory chapter, being explored here at greater depth and as a means of reflecting on this book's contents:

Superficial rote learning, with assessment based on factual recall, should be minimized

In response to the agenda set by high stakes external examinations, many teachers tend to mirror such tests and other forms of summative assessment in their classrooms – ostensibly to prepare students for GCSEs, AS and A level examinations. However, they often struggle to devise tests that are valid and reliable, creating assessments that mostly test the recall of factual knowledge, much of which is subsequently forgotten by their students. Student motivation is often decreased, while the formation of deeper knowledge and understanding becomes sidelined. When used on a regular basis in classrooms, summative assessment encourages students to learn by rote – prompting them to develop superficial knowledge rather than long-term, deeper understanding. This can be a hindrance to progression as students merely accumulate chunks of facts, rather than seeing how their knowledge and understanding should fit together. This is a poor foundation on which to build new learning, for students see their short-term test results as the end-point of the educational process, rather than as a stepping stone to the next phase of their learning. Higher order thinking skills – such as analysis, evaluation and reasoned decision-making – are often absent from such testing regimes. This creates problems for students who have previously performed well in pencil and paper tests, but who subsequently struggle when assessment demands are changed (Butt 2006e).

Teachers fail to review and reflect upon the types of assessment they use and do not discuss these with colleagues

Assessment in the classroom has, until recently, often been a rather closed, restricted and personal activity that has defied clear description and analysis. In many schools and departments it remains so. To a substantial number of teachers assessment is simply a necessary 'evil' – a time-consuming but ultimately fairly fruitless task which 'the system' demands. Many teachers simply get on with it, but do not want to invest additional time and effort into reforming or exploring what they do with respect to assessment. This situation is changing through the implementation of policy initiatives, professional development, training, and the influence of school inspections, which promote AfL in the classroom. However, it is important that teachers talk to each other about their assessment practices and agree to make changes together – without the support of colleagues, taking appropriate action becomes an uphill struggle (Butt 2006e).

Teacher assessment overemphasizes grading, but underemphasizes learning

Teachers have to be very careful about what sort of assessment information they feed back to students. If comments, grades or marks are released carelessly they can be damaging and de-motivational (see Harlen 2008c), or can send incorrect messages about what is valued and about how to improve. If feedback comments are typified by unfocused praise (or censure) they do not help the learner improve; when students cannot reason why their work has been rewarded with lavish praise (or damned by withering criticism) they will not understand how to perform better. By being well intentioned, but indiscriminate, teachers can send confusing messages to students about their performance and attainment.

There is still an over-emphasis in many classrooms on grading students' work, while the clear signalling of the next steps to take with respect to learning is generally under-emphasized. A way forward is to base assessment comments on commonly understood performance criteria. This has the advantage of both teacher and learner talking the same assessment language, while progressive criteria form a hierarchy of statements which make the ways forward apparent. Obviously a criterion statement will give much more information than a single grade or numerical mark – if necessary a level might be recorded in a mark book or electronic file to give an approximate short-hand reference to performance. An assessment system that relies just on teachers' comments, or solely on grades, will not be able to provide a richness of information to feed back to teachers and learners (Butt 2006e).

Assessment systems tend to be norm-, rather than criterion-, referenced

Despite the assessment of National Curriculum subjects, in part, being criterion-referenced against Level Descriptions, there is still a dominance of norm-referenced systems of assessment in schools. Where teacher assessment is the only method by which students are awarded levels, the assessment system is usually criterion-referenced. However, many teachers still place their faith in normative assessments to determine each student's level of achievement. There are examples of teachers 'disaggregating' level descriptions into their component parts, which are then assessed through exercises, tests or exams. Single end-of-year exams, or other one-off assessment events, may also be over-used to provide a summative level for the student's attainment. Level descriptions are more complex than this and are not designed to be used in this way. They are statements of multiple knowledge, understanding and skills that cannot be accurately assessed by a single test event. The belief that norm-referenced assessment is the most objective and reliable means of assessment is misplaced (Butt 2006e).

Teachers emphasize competition through their assessment methods, rather than personal achievement and performance

Norm-referenced assessment, based on an end-of-unit or -year test, is usually designed with the purpose of rank ordering students' performance – essentially to give information about how one student's performance compares with another's. Students understand such assessment events as being straightforward competitions: there is little other interpretation for a system that is designed to rank and grade their performance. This can be motivational to those students who regularly perform well, but is frustrating and de-motivational to those who do not. These students are left with little idea of how to improve, as the ranking/grading is often the end point of the assessment process. Usually there is little emphasis placed on personal achievement, certainly not in the form that helps students take the next steps towards improving their learning (Butt 2006e).

Assessment methods tend to reinforce perceptions of failure amongst the less able

Over-reliance on summative assessment can be confidence-sapping for many students. Regular hierarchical ordering of student performance means that less able students give up, as they are left with little confidence in their ability to learn. All that assessment does for such students is to reinforce their sense of failure, telling them what they can't do rather than what they can. These students regularly feel helpless, seeing little incentive to engage in an education system that rewards them so frugally. Learners need to be given a sense of achievement, confidence and self-esteem from the assessment methods they are subjected to (Butt 2006e).

Dominance of external, summative testing

As external assessment still dominates the assessment system, teachers become very experienced in understanding the structure, demands and types of questions that examination papers will contain. Arguably, they may understand the examination set-up better than they know their own students' learning needs – although it is impressive how accurately many teachers can predict the likely grades that individual students will attain at the point of final assessment. But there can be problems with this – if the teacher predicts that a student (or group of students) will almost certainly achieve a particular grade in their GCSE, then a degree of complacency may creep in. This can develop into a self-fulfilling prophecy. There are additional, associated dangers if we mostly target our efforts into ensuring that potentially borderline candidates raise their grades to the next level/grade when assessed. Without realistic, careful target-setting, the performance of many students may be held at an expected, rather than an ultimately achievable, level (Butt 2006e).

Over-emphasis on quantity and presentation of students' work

There is a concern, often associated with 'impression marking', that teachers award higher marks to those students whose written work appears to be longer and more neatly presented than others. This form of superficial assessment is usually linked to secondary school teachers whose weekly marking load may be exceptionally high, tempting them into 'tick and flick' marking techniques. Here the assessment of quality may be reduced to a crude judgement of the length and neatness of a student's work, or a judgement about whether they have simply finished a set task. This can be damaging to the student, for a high grade may be awarded to a piece of work which actually has rather modest academic merit (Butt 2006e).

Essentially there are no quick or easy solutions to these common assessment problems (Black and Wiliam 1998b). Nonetheless there is also a danger of labelling all 'traditional' assessment practices negatively, while reifying 'progressive' ways forward. What has become clear is that there is no single solution to all our assessment issues; simply being aware that problems persist and need addressing is a good start (Butt 2006e).

It is possible to condense many of the current weaknesses associated with day-to-day assessment into eight, short bullet points. These points, originally stated in Black *et al.*'s (2003) account of their work on assessment in schools during a two-year project in Medway and Oxfordshire – the King's, Medway, Oxfordshire Formative Assessment Project (KMOFAP) – are arranged under three subheadings: effective learning, negative impact and managerial roles of assessment.

Effective Learning

◆ Teachers' tests encourage rote and superficial learning; this is seen even where teachers say they want to develop understanding – and many appear unaware of the inconsistency.
◆ The questions and other methods used are not discussed with or shared between teachers in the same school, and they are not critically reviewed in relation to what they actually assess.
◆ For primary teachers in particular, there is a tendency to emphasize quantity and presentation of work and to neglect its quality in relation to learning.

Negative Impact

◆ The giving of marks and grading functions are over-emphasized, while the giving of useful advice and the learning function are under-emphasized.
◆ The use of approaches in which students are compared with one another, the prime purpose of which appears to them to be competition rather than personal improvement. In consequence, assessment feedback teaches students with low attainments that they lack 'ability', so they are de-motivated, believing that they are not able to learn.

Managerial Role

◆ Teachers' feedback to students often appears to serve social and managerial functions, often at the expense of the learning functions.
◆ Teachers are often able to predict students' results on external tests – because their own tests imitate them – but at the same time they know too little about their students' learning needs.
◆ The collection of marks to fill up records is given greater priority

than the analysis of students' work to discern learning needs; furthermore, some teachers pay no attention to the assessment records of previous teachers of their students. (Black *et al.* 2003, p. 11)

This brings us back to the adage of 'assessing less, better'. If teachers reduce their marking load, targeting it to the future educational needs of the students, they gain the space to improve their assessment practice. There is no imperative to mark everything to the same depth or standard. Much of what students write in the classroom is completed under our direct guidance – it may contain little new, valuable assessment information. Better that we plan key assessment events carefully, which we can be confident will provide us with insights on students' performance that can be usefully fed back to help them improve. The skill in marking such assessments is more advanced, requiring better planning and targeted time to assess, to ensure that the outcome helps to support students' learning.

A warning – the persistence of high stakes testing

Despite the acknowledgement of the importance of formative assessment, and the recognition that over-use of summative testing and assessment methods in the classroom can damage students' educational progress, the influence of the latter still persists strongly in many schools. In April 2009, the BBC Education website ran a feature entitled 'Schools keep testing 14-year-olds' which revealed that hundreds of thousands of 14-year-olds in England would still face SATs testing, despite their abolition earlier in the year. Although such testing was no longer compulsory, the majority of schools (3,283 of the 4,186 which were subject to statutory testing in the previous year) still requested to be sent test papers for Maths and English assessment from the QCDA. These tests are still produced by the QCDA, alongside other optional tests, and are annually requested by a substantial number of schools. It appears that although many teachers are opposed to the over-assessment of their students through summative means, a significant number are not – perhaps influenced by senior management teams who have built their assessment systems around the regular input of SATs results and other high stakes assessment data. There are also possibilities that some parents trust uch evidence of their children's progress, and that a substantial proportion of teachers still believe that SATs-type testing is a convenient and accurate way of assessing their students' progress.

A strong and persistent high stakes, summative assessment culture therefore still exists within schools, which may take many years to shift given the evidence of schools' insistence on maintaining testing regimes, even when SATs have been abolished.

Conclusions

The concept of formative assessment has developed and strengthened in recent years. Although many use the terms 'assessment for learning' and 'formative assessment' interchangeably, there are subtle differences in the assessment practices associated with them. For example, Black *et al.* (2003) point out that for some teachers formative assessment means frequent informal testing (or 'micro summative' assessment), whereas for others it implies informal assessment limited to the purpose of improving learning – 'yet formal testing can be used to improve learning and to serve more than one purpose, while informal assessment can be used for summative purposes' (p. 122). They also note that formative assessment can at times be formative for the teacher, but not for the student!

It all depends on what we understand by the learning process. In the British educational system most teachers would not agree that their role is simply that of a 'curriculum deliverer'; they want to instil a love of learning in their students alongside their ability to be autonomous, self-motivated and stimulated by education. Establishing life-long learners, capable of independent reasoning and problem-solving, is considered a major goal by many teachers. These are, after all, the necessary skills of the modern age. In our rapidly changing world, young people need to be flexible and adaptable. They need to be good self-starters, organized, rational, intellectually skilled and able to meet their own learning and developmental goals. Our assessment system must prepare students for these demands. In a world where risks must be weighed and responded to, where resilience and fortitude are important, our education and assessment system must prepare young people to cope and excel. Fostering appropriate attitudes to learning is the key, while recognizing that assessment is a significant component of this.

To summarize, the main guiding principles for assessment can be stated as follows:

◆ Identify your assessment objectives when you are planning your lessons; make assessment integral to teaching and learning.
◆ Be clear about how these objectives will be met (e.g. what assessment methods you will use, what acceptable performance will look like, etc.).
◆ Communicate your assessment objectives to the students, in a language which they can all understand.
◆ Be focused in your assessment of students' work; know what you are looking for and why.
◆ Communicate your findings to students in good time; identify the gap between current performance and desired goals, highlight misconceptions, common errors, etc.
◆ Identify how students' performance can be improved; give students the opportunity to self- and peer assess.
◆ Integrate your assessment findings into future planning and teaching.

Additionally, Swaffield (2008) rightly concludes that:

◆ Assessment reflects what we value.
◆ Assessment should be aligned with our beliefs about learning.
◆ The prime purpose of assessment is to assist learning, helping young people grow as learners.
◆ The quality of assessment determines the quality of the conclusions we draw.
◆ Practice should be guided by principles. (p. 174)

It is clear that assessment serves a number of purposes in our schools and that external, summative assessment still exerts a controlling influence on what happens in most classrooms. Ensuring that summative and formative assessment remain in equilibrium is essential for 'the present balance struck between the two is unhealthy, and has shifted even more in recent years to negate the potential benefits of varied learning and assessment experiences' (Lambert and Lines 2000, p. 198). Teachers have an important role to play in ensuring that the correct assessment balance is maintained, although the role of the researcher is also significant in theorizing the role of educational assessment. It is worthwhile, finally, to remind ourselves of the overall purposes to which we put our assessment regimes, the effects that these have on the curriculum, and the need to maintain an enquiring approach to help us understand the complex relationships between assessment and learning. Jim Ridgway and Sean McCusker express this very effectively:

> Assessment is central to educational practice. High-stakes assessments exemplify curriculum ambitions, define what is worth knowing, and drive classroom practices. It is essential to develop systems for assessment which reflect our core educational goals, and which reward students for developing skills and attributes which will be of long-term benefit to them and to society. There is good research evidence to show that well-designed assessment systems lead to improved student performance. (Ridgway, McCusker and Read 2004)

References

Angoff, W. H. (1988) 'Validity: an evolving concept', in Linn, R. L. (ed.) *Educational Measurement* (3rd edn). Washington DC: American Council on Education/Macmillan.

Arnot, M., Gray, J., James, M., Rudduck, J. with Duveen, G. (1998) *Recent Research on Gender and Educational Performance*. London: Stationery Office.

Assessment Reform Group (1999) *Assessment for Learning: Beyond the Black Box*. Cambridge: University of Cambridge, Faculty of Education.

—— (2002) *Ten Principles of Assessment for Learning*. Cambridge: University of Cambridge.

Asthana, A. (2009) 'GCSEs blamed for boys not going to university', *The Observer*, 7 June, p. 18.

Bekhradnia, B. (2009) 'Tear up these exams or we're going to leave our boys behind', *The Observer*, 7 June, p. 27.

Black, P., Harrison, C., Lee, C., Marshall, B. and Wiliam, D. (2002) *Working Inside the Black Box: Assessment for Learning in the Classroom*. London: Kings College.

—— (2003) *Assessment for Learning: Putting it into Practice*. Maidenhead: Open University Press.

Black, P. and Wiliam, D. (1998a) 'Assessment and classroom learning', *Assessment in Education*, 5, pp. 7–74.

—— (1998b) *Inside the Black Box: Raising Standards Through Classroom Assessment*. London: King's College.

—— (2003) '"In Praise of Educational Research": formative assessment', *British Educational Research Journal*, 29(5), pp. 623–37.

—— (2008a) 'The reliability of assessments', in Gardner, J. (ed.) (2008) *Assessment and Learning*. London: Sage, pp. 119–31.

—— (2008b) 'Assessment for learning in the classroom', in Gardner, J. (ed.) (2008) *Assessment and Learning*. London: Sage, pp. 9–25.

Black, P. and Wiliam, D. (2008c) 'Developing a theory of formative assessment', in Gardner, J. (ed.) (2008) *Assessment and Learning*. London: Sage, pp. 81–100.

Bleach, K. (ed.) (2000) *Raising Boys' Achievement in Schools*. Stoke on Trent: Trentham.

Bloom, B. S., Hastings, J. T. and Madaus, G. F. (eds) (1971) *Handbook on the Formative and Summative Evaluation of Student Learning*. New York: McGraw Hill.

Board of Education (1933) *Report of the Consultative Committee on Infant and Nursery Schools (Hadow Report)*. London: HMSO.

Boardman, D. (1990) 'Graphicacy revisited: mapping abilities and gender differences', *Educational Review*, 42(1), pp. 57–64.

Boston, K. (2005) *Strategy, Technology and Assessment*, presentation to Round Table Conference, Melbourne, Australia.

Bradley-Smith, P. (2002) 'Closing the gender gap in geography: update 2 – "invisible" girls', *Teaching Geography*, July, pp. 143–6.

Brooks, V. (2002) *Assessment in Secondary Schools: the new teacher's guide to monitoring, assessment, recording and reporting*. Buckingham: Open University Press.

Bruner, J. (1961) *The Process of Education*. Cambridge, MA: Harvard University Press.

Butler, R. (1988) 'Enhancing and undermining intrinsic motivation: the effects of task–involving and ego involving evaluation on interest and performance', *British Journal of Educational Psychology*, 58, pp. 1–14.

Butt, G. (2001) 'Closing the gender gap in geography', *Teaching Geography*, 26(3), pp. 145–7.

—— (2002) *Reflective Teaching of Geography 11–18*. London: Continuum.

—— (2005a) 'A first look at assessment', *Into Teaching*, 1(2), pp. 3–5.

—— (2005b) '"High Stakes" or "Low Stakes" assessment?', *Into Teaching*, 1(3), pp. 14–16.

—— (2005c) 'Marking, marking, marking', *Into Teaching*, 1(4), pp. 15–17.

—— (2006a) 'How does theory inform practice in assessment?', *Into Teaching*, 1(2), pp. 19–21.

—— (2006b) 'Using assessment to support students' learning', *Into Teaching – the induction year*, 1(13), pp. 15–20.

—— (2006c) 'What are marks used for?', *Into Teaching*, 1(6), pp. 15–17.

Butt, G. (2006d) 'Setting – and getting – assessment targets', *Into Teaching – the induction year*, 1(15), pp. 14–18.

—— (2006e) 'Enhancing the quality of assessment', *Into Teaching*, 1(7), pp. 14–16.

Butt, G. with Bradley-Smith, P. and Woods, P. (2006) 'Gender issues in geography', in Balderstone, D. (ed.) *Secondary Geography Handbook*. Sheffield: Geographical Association, pp. 384–93.

Butt, G. and Gunter, H. (2007) 'Remodelling learning – the use of technology', in Butt, G. and Gunter, H. (eds) (2007) *Modernizing Schools: people, learning and organizations*. London: Continuum, pp. 105–17.

Butt, G. and Lance, A. (2005) 'Secondary teacher workload and job satisfaction – do successful strategies for change exist?', *Educational Management Administration and Leadership*, 33(4), pp. 401–22.

Butt, G. and Smith, P. (1998) 'Educational standards and assessment in geography – some cause for concern?', *Teaching Geography*, 23(3), pp. 147–9.

Butt, G., Weeden, P. and Wood, P. (2004) 'Boys' underachievement in geography: a question of ability, attitude or assessment?', *International Research in Geographical and Environmental Education*, 13(4), pp. 329–47.

Carr, M. (2001) *Assessment in Early Childhood Settings*. London: Paul Chapman Publishing.

—— (2008) 'Can assessment unlock and open the doors to resourcefulness and agency?', in Swaffield, S. (ed.) (2008) *Unlocking Assessment: understanding for reflection and application*. Abingdon: Routledge, pp. 36–54.

Chitty, C. (2001) 'IQ, racism and the eugenics movement', *Forum*, 43, pp. 115–20.

Clarke, S. (1998) *Targeting Assessment in the Primary School*. London: Hodder and Stoughton.

—— (2001) *Unlocking Formative Assessment: practical strategies for enhancing pupil's learning in the primary classroom*. Abingdon: Hodder Education.

Dann, R. (2002) *Promoting Assessment as Learning: improving the learning process*. London: RoutledgeFalmer.

Delamont, S. (1999) 'Gender and the discourse of derision', *Research Papers in Education*, 14, pp. 3–21.

Dewey, J. (1916) *Democracy and Education: an introduction to the philosophy of education*. New York: Free Press.

DCSF (2007) *National Curriculum Assessments at Key Stage 3 in England 2007 (Provisional)* (National Statistics: First Release). London: HMSO.

DfES/QCA (2002) *Key Stage 3 Strategy: Training Materials for the Foundation Subjects.* London: HMSO.

DfES (2004a) *Key Stage 3 Strategy: Assessment for Learning: whole school training materials.* London: HMSO.

—— (2004b) *Unit 6: Curricular Target Setting.* London: DfES.

—— (2005) *Harnessing Technology: transforming learning and children's services.* London: HMSO.

Drummond, M. J. (2008) 'Assessment and values: a close and necessary relationship', in Swaffield, S. (ed.) *Unlocking Assessment: understanding for reflection and application.* Abingdon: Routledge, pp. 3–19.

Dudley and Swaffield, S. (2008) 'Understanding and using assessment data', in Swaffield, S. (ed.) *Unlocking Assessment: understanding for reflection and application.* Abingdon: Routledge, pp. 105–20.

Dweck, C. S. (1999) *Self-theories: their role in motivation, personality and development.* Philadelphia, PA: Hove Psychology Press.

Ecclestone, K. and Pryor, J. (2003) '"Learning careers" or "Assessment careers"? The impact of assessment systems on learning', *British Educational Research Journal*, 29(4), pp. 471–88.

Epstein, D., Elwood, J., Hey, V. and Maw, J. (eds) (1998) *Failing Boys?: Issues in gender and achievement.* Buckingham: Open University Press.

Filer, A. and Pollard, A. (2000) *The Social World of Student Assessment.* London: Continuum.

Flinders, K. and Flinders, E. (2000) 'Long term, summative assessment and evaluation', in Hopkin, J., Telfer, S. and Butt, G. (eds) *Assessment in Practice.* Sheffield: Geographical Association, pp. 71–9.

Foster, V., Kimmel, M. and Skelton, C. (2001) 'What about the boys? An overview of debate', in Martino, W. and Meyenn, C. (eds) *What About the Boys?* Buckingham: Open University Press.

Francis, B. (2000) *Boys, Girls and Achievement: addressing the classroom issues.* London: Routledge.

Gardner, J. (ed.) (2008) *Assessment and Learning.* London: Sage.

Gillborn, D. and Mirza, H. (2000) *Educational Inequality: mapping race, class and gender, a synthesis of research evidence.* London: OfSTED.

Glaser, R. (1963) 'Instructional technology and the measurement of learning outcomes', *American Psychologist*, 18, pp. 510–22.

Gorard, S. (2001) 'International comparisons of school effectiveness: a second component of the "crisis account"?', *Comparative Education*, 37(2), pp. 279–96.

—— (2002) 'Fostering scepticism: the importance of warranting claims', *Evaluation and Research in Education*, 16(3), pp. 136–49.

—— (2005) 'Academies as the "future of schooling": is this an evidence-based policy?', *Journal of Education Policy*, 20(3), pp. 369–77.

—— (2008) 'The value-added of primary schools: what is it really measuring?', *Educational Review*, 60(2), pp. 179–85.

—— (2010) 'Serious doubts about school effectiveness', *British Educational Research Journal* (issue not given).

Gorard, S., with Adnett, N., May, H., Slack, K., Smith, E. and Thomas, L. (2007) *Overcoming the Barriers to Higher Education*. Stoke on Trent: Trentham Books.

Gorard, S., Rees, G. and Salisbury, J. (1999) 'Reappraising the apparent underachievement of boys at school', *Gender and Education*, 11, pp. 441–54.

Gorard, S. and Smith, E. (2004) 'What is "underachievement"?', *School Leadership and Management*, 24(2), pp. 205–25.

Hargreaves, E. (2005) 'Assessment for learning? Thinking outside the (black) box', *Cambridge Journal of Education*, 35(2), pp. 213–24.

Harlen, W. (2008a) 'Trusting teachers' judgement', in Swaffield, S. (ed.), *Unlocking Assessment: understanding for reflection and application*. Abingdon: Routledge.

—— (2008b) 'On the relationship between assessment for formative and summative purposes', in Gardner, J. (ed.) *Assessment and Learning*. London: Sage, pp. 103–17.

—— (2008c) 'The role of assessment in developing motivation for learning', in Gardner, J. (ed.) *Assessment and Learning*. London: Sage, pp. 61–80.

Hart, S., Dixon, A., Drummond, M.-J. and McIntyre, D. (2004) *Learning Without Limits*. Maidenhead: Open University Press.

Hodgen, J. and Webb, M. (2008) 'Questioning and dialogue', in Swaffield, S. (ed.) *Unlocking Assessment: understanding for reflection and application*. Abingdon: Routledge, pp. 73–89.

Jackson, C. (2002) 'Can single-sex classes in co-educational schools enhance the learning experiences of girls and/or boys? An exploration of students' perceptions', *British Educational Research Journal*, 28(1), pp. 37–48.

Jackson, C. (2003) 'Motives for "laddishness" at school: fear of failure and fear of the feminine', *British Educational Research Journal*, 29(4), pp. 583–98.

James, M. (2008a) 'Assessment and learning', in Swaffield, S. (ed.), *Unlocking Assessment: understanding for reflection and application*. Abingdon: Routledge, pp. 20–35.

—— (2008b) 'Assessment, teaching and theories of learning', in Gardner, J. (ed.) *Assessment and Learning*. London: Sage, pp. 47–60.

Jenkins, S. (2008) 'All this public waste is born of a macho bigness fixation', *The Guardian*, 17 December 2008.

JISC/QCA (2006) *e-Assessment Glossary (extended)*. London: JISC/QCA.

John, P. (2005) 'The sacred and the profane: subject sub-culture, pedagogical practice and teachers' perceptions of the classroom use of ICT', *Educational Review*, 57(4), pp. 471–90.

Joint Information Systems Committee (JISC) (2006) *Briefing Paper: e-assessment: an overview of JISC activities*. London: JISC.

Lambert, D. (1996) 'Assessing students' attainment and supporting learning', in Kent, A., Lambert, D., Naish, M. and Slater, F. (eds) *Geography in Education*. Cambridge: CUP, pp. 260–87.

Lambert, D. and Lines, D. (2000) *Understanding Assessment: purposes, perceptions, practice*. London: RoutledgeFalmer.

Madaus, G. (1988) 'The influence of testing on the curriculum', in Tanner, L. (ed.), *Critical Issues in Curriculum*. Chicago: University of Chicago Press, pp. 83–121.

Martino, W. (1999) '"Cool boys", "Party Animals", "Squids" and "Poofters": interrogating the dynamics and politics of adolescent masculinities in school', *British Journal of Sociology of Education*, 20(2), pp. 239–63.

OfSTED (2003) *Good Assessment in Secondary Schools*. London: Stationery Office.

—— (2008) *Assessment for Learning: the impact of National Strategy support*. London: Stationery Office.

Olson, J. (2000) 'Trojan horse or teachers' pet? Computers and the culture of schools', *Journal of Curriculum Studies*, 31(1), pp. 1–9.

Piaget, J. (1954) *Origins of Intelligence in Children*. New York: International Universities Press.

Pollard, A. and Filer, A. (1999) *The Social World of Student Career: strategic biographies through primary school*. London: Cassell.

QCA (2005) 'A proposed blueprint for e-assessment', http://www.qca.org.uk.

—— (2008) 'e-assessment', http://www.qca.org.uk.

Reay, D. and Wiliam, D. (1999) '"I'll be a nothing": structure, agency and the construction of identity through assessment', *British Educational Research Journal*, 25, pp. 343–54.

Ridgway, J., McCusker, S. and Read, D. (2004) *Literature Review of E-assessment. Report 10: Futurelab Series*. Bristol: Futurelab.

Ripley, M. (2007) *E Assessment – an update on research, policy and practice. Report 10 Update: Futurelab Series*. Bristol: Futurelab.

—— (2008) 'Technology in the service of twenty-first century learning and assessment', in Swaffield, S. (ed.), *Unlocking Assessment: understanding for reflection and application*. Abingdon: Routledge, pp. 154–72.

Rynne, E. (2009) 'What are the challenges of e-assessment?', in Weeden, P. and Butt, G. (eds), *Assessing Progress in Your Key Stage 3 Geography Curriculum*. Sheffield: Geographical Association, pp. 39–45.

Sadler, R. (1989) 'Formative assessment and the design of instructional systems', *Instructional Science*, 18, pp. 119–44.

Schagen, I. (2006) 'The use of standardised residuals to derive value-added measures of school performance', *Educational Studies*, 32(2), pp. 119–32.

Scriven, M. (1967) *The Methodology of Evaluation*. Washington, DC: American Educational Research Association.

Smith, E. (2005) *Analysing Underachievement in Schools*. London: Continuum.

—— (2008) 'Matter of debate: understanding underachievement', *Curriculum Briefing*, 6(2), pp. 6–8.

Stobart, G. (2008) *Testing Times: The uses and abuses of assessment*.

Sukhnandan, L., Lee, B. and Kelleher, S. (2000) *An Investigation into Gender Differences in Achievement. Phase 2: School and classroom strategies*. Slough: NFER.

London: Routledge.

Sutton, R. (1995) *Assessment: A Framework for Teachers*. Windsor: NFER-Nelson.

Swaffield, S. (2008) 'Continuing the exploration', in Swaffield, S. (ed.) *Unlocking Assessment: understanding for reflection and application*. Abingdon: Routledge, pp. 173–4.

Torrance, H. and Pryor, J. (1998) *Investigating Formative Assessment: teaching learning and assessment in the classroom.* Buckingham: Open University Press.

Tunstall, P. and Gipps, C. (1996) 'Teacher feedback to young children in formative assessment: a typology', *British Educational Research Journal*, 22(4), pp. 389–404.

Vygotsky, L. (1962) *Thought and Language.* Cambridge, MA: MIT Press.

Warrington, M. and Younger, M. (1999) 'Perspectives on the gender gap in English secondary schools', *Research Papers in Education*, 14, pp. 51–77.

Weeden, P., Winter, J. and Broadfoot, P. (2002) *Assessment: what's in it for schools?* London: RoutledgeFalmer.

Wiliam, D. (2001) 'Reliability, validity and all that jazz', *Education 3–13*, 29, pp. 17–21.

—— (2008) 'Quality in assessment', in Swaffield, S. (ed.) *Unlocking Assessment: understanding for reflection and application.* Abingdon: Routledge, pp. 123–37.

Wood, P. (2002) 'Closing the gender gap in geography: update 1', *Teaching Geography*, 27(1), pp. 41–3.

Younger, M., Warrington, M. and Williams, J. (1999) 'The gender gap and classroom interactions: reality and rhetoric?', *British Journal of Sociology of Education*, 20(3), pp. 325–42.

Index